*Getting Your*
## Beauty

# Getting Jobs in Beauty

**Lesley Moore**

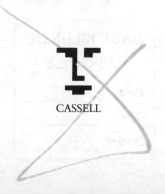

CASSELL

Cassell Publishers Limited
Artillery House, Artillery Row
London SW1P 1RT

© Lesley Moore 1988

First published 1988

**British Library Cataloguing in Publication Data**

Moore, Lesley
Getting jobs in beauty.
1. Beauty care – Career guides
I. Title
646.7′2′023

ISBN 0 304 31482 X

Some occupations, titles, phrases or individual words in this publication
may refer to a worker or workers of a particular sex, but they should not be
taken to imply that the occupation or career is restricted to one sex, unless
the occupation is excluded from the general provisions of the Sex
Discrimination Act.

The views expressed in this book are those of the author and not necessarily
those of the Inner London Education Authority.

Typeset by Scribe Design, Gillingham, Kent
Printed and bound in Great Britain by
Billings Book Plan Ltd, Worcester

# Contents

# Contents

# Contents

# Who is This Book For?

- If you think you may be interested in pursuing a career in the beauty industry this book will help you find out more about what is involved. It will help you to make important decisions about your future and could save you from a wrong decision which would make you unhappy later on.

- If you have already decided beauty is for you and have organized an interview at a college to study beauty therapy, this book will help you prepare the right questions to ask. It may even help you obtain a place.

  It will tell you who the employers are and what they look for, and you will hear from people who are already doing jobs in this field. It will give you a flavour of the industry to help you decide if it the one for you.

- If you are a parent you may wish to read this book in order to help your son or daughter make the right career decision. It is intended to give the information you need to assist your children with their research into what is best for their future. You may like to use this book along with others in the series when you are talking to your children.

- If you are a Careers Adviser you can use this book during vocational guidance interviews to ensure that the information you give is up to date. The book goes into the beauty industry in far greater depth than you will be able to during your initial contact with the client; therefore you might like to refer your client to it if they wish to undertake further research.

  You could also use it as part a of group information session on the beauty industry. The quizzes in the book may be a good introduction to such a session.

- If you are a careers teacher in a school or college you will find this book a useful addition to your careers library. It will be a good reference point for those young people contemplating a career in the beauty industry. You will be able to use it as part of your career lessons or when you are trying to find out more for a motivated young person.

- If you are contemplating changing your career or are about to take up a career in middle life, you will find this book of value. It will inform you about the options open to you and will give you a true insight into the industry. It should help you as you make an important career decision, and it will direct you towards other agencies who can help you.

- It is possible that you are already involved in one aspect of the beauty industry. Maybe you are already a beauty therapist and are beginning to look at what prospects there are for you. This book can help you, too. It will give you ideas about the choice of pathways open to you in your present position. Perhaps you are considering opening your own business? Read on – points on starting are detailed inside.

# How to Use This Book

## Method 1

This book has been written in a way that will allow you to dip into the parts that interest you the most. It will guide you to the areas that will be most helpful to you so that you do not necessarily have to read the book from cover to cover.

There are a number of quizzes in the book to give you an introduction to each career area; try them. They will help you to decide if you need to read the rest of that section.

The first quiz is at the beginning of the book. Start with this: it will lead you to a starting-point most appropriate to your needs.

## Method 2

If you have already decided that the beauty industry is for you and are wanting to find out more about the job you have chosen, then you can turn immediately to the chapters about that job. You may find mention of other jobs where the skills required are similar. If so, you should read these other chapters before you make your final decision.

## Method 3

If you are completely new to the industry and are coming to it with an open mind, I suggest you read the book all the way through. It will be valuable in helping you make your decision; it will also be valuable if you need to advise others in their career choices.

# The Career Pathway for You

The 'Career Pathway in Beauty Chart' shows the different entry points for the beauty industry. Some career choices involve further training, others allow you to learn your skills while you are working. Look at the employment column, find the job title that most

**?**

attracts you, then follow the pathway and see where it leads. You may find the career pathway you have chosen involves a training course. To help you decide which part of this book you should read first and what action you should take next, answer the questions below.

1. *Do you have any qualifications? If not, are you prepared to get some?*

   *Yes* Continue to the next question.

   *No* Turn to the chapters entitled
   Manicurists   p.78
   Masseurs/Masseuses   p.92
   Make-up Artists   p.94
   Colour Consultants   p.106
   Cosmetic Sales   p.109

2. *Are you prepared to consider a full-time course to train you in your chosen career?*

   *No* Only a part-time course – turn to the chapters entitled
   Manicurists   p.78
   Alternative Therapists   p.84
   Masseurs/Masseuses   p.92
   (Full-time courses are also available.)

   *Yes* Turn to the chapters entitled
   Beauty Therapy   p.13
   Beauticians   p.75
   Make-up Artists   p.94

3. *Are you already trained as a beauty therapist and now looking for alternatives?*

   *No* Return to questions 1 and 2 above.

   *Yes* Turn to the chapters entitled
   What are the Prospects?   p.59
   Alternative Therapists   p.84
   Masseurs/Masseuses   p.92
   Make-up Artists   p.94

4. *Are you an adult considering embarking on a new career or about to begin a career?*

   *No* Return to questions 1, 2 or 3 above.

   *Yes* Read on.

**5.** *Are you prepared to consider full-time training?*

No   Return to questions 1 and 2 above.

Yes  Read Part One of the book, paying particular attention to the
     chapter entitled 'Opportunities for Job Changers'
     Then turn to the chapters entitled
     Beauticians   p.75
     Alternative Therapists   p.84
     Masseurs/Masseuses   p.92
     Make-up Artists   p.94

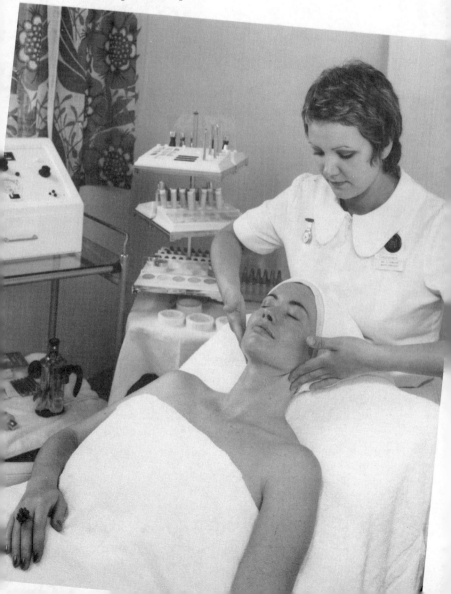

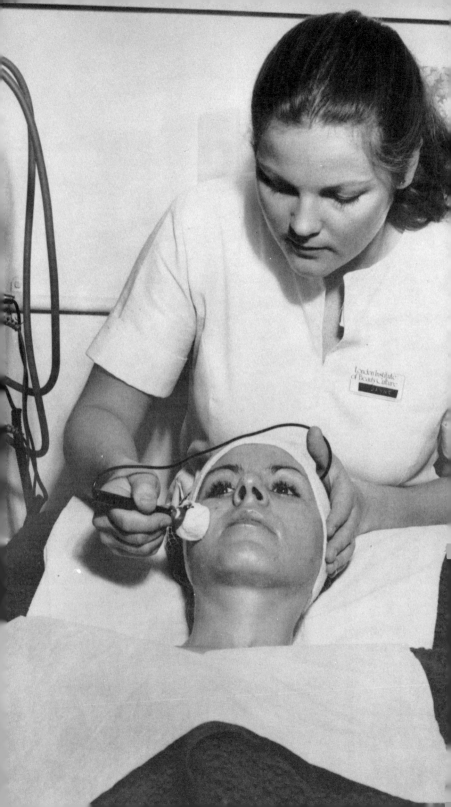

# PART ONE
# BEAUTY THERAPY

# What do You Know About Beauty Therapy?

There are some jobs that we are familiar with, perhaps because our parents or friends do them or because every day we encounter people doing them. For instance, we are familiar with the job of sales assistants; we all meet them at some point when we go shopping. We have a good idea of what a sales assistant's job involves even if we don't have the full story.

Beauty therapy is a different matter. It conjures up all sorts of pictures in people's minds because a beauty salon is not a place that most of us visit on a regular basis.

The first part of this book introduces you to the world of beauty therapy. But first see how much you really know by answering the quiz below.

| STATEMENT | TRUE | FALSE |
|---|---|---|
| 1  The most popular treatment offered by a beauty therapist is the application of make-up. | | |
| 2  All beauty therapists train on the job. | | |
| 3  Most beauty therapists work in health resorts. | | |
| 4  A beauty therapist's clients are normally models or actresses. | | |
| 5  Most beauty therapists become make-up artists. | | |

# BEAUTY THERAPY

## Formal Career Pathways

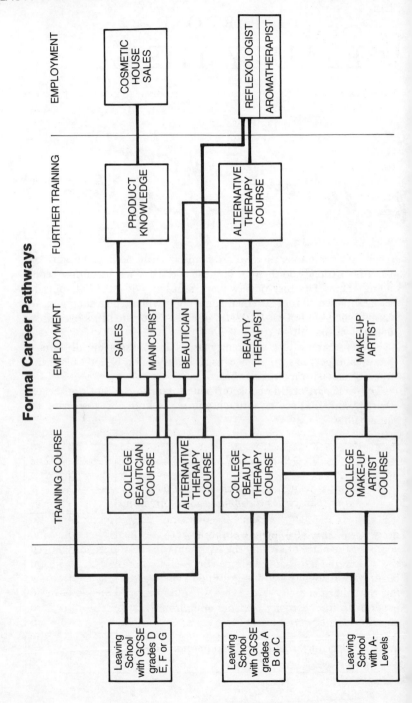

# 2
# The People

I would like to take this opportunity to introduce you to some people I met while I was writing this book. They are all people who are involved in some way in the beauty industry, and those you will meet in the next few pages have made their careers as beauty therapists. Later on I will introduce you to people who are linked with the beauty world in other ways.

In the introductions you will find out a little about their backgrounds and how they got to where they are today. They are people who have been in the same position as you.

They will comment on being involved in beauty therapy throughout Part One of the book, thus building up a picture of what beauty therapy is really like.

## Introducing Joanne

Joanne Blastland is twenty-five years old. She trained to be a beauty therapist at the Abraham Moss Open College in Manchester. It is a futher education college where Jo took her City and Guilds qualification during a two-year course. At that time it was necessary to be at least eighteen years old to start a course, so Jo stayed on at school after her O-levels (she passed seven) to take A-levels in Biology and English.

Jo was not sure what she wanted to do when she left school so she spoke to her Careers Officer. They discussed her interests and the Careers Officer suggested that either physiotherapy or beauty therapy might be worth considering. Jo visited the local hospital and spent some time in the physiotherapy department. She discovered that she did not have the patience required for the job, so she pursued the idea of beauty therapy and decided that it was what she wanted to do. It seemed an interesting option offering many things she enjoyed.

Having obtained places at three further education colleges, Jo decided that it would be more economical to stay nearer her home and accepted the place offered by the Abraham Moss College. She enjoyed the course and felt that it equipped her well for her first job, in a local beauty salon, which she found through a friend. At the same time she felt that she was lucky, because it was difficult for someone with no experience to find their first job. After ten months she moved to another high street salon in Manchester which employed two staff. All her subsequent jobs have been found by writing to salons in the area in which she wanted to work. She found the addresses in telephone directories.

A trip abroad ended her second job, and when she returned she found a job in a hotel that had a sauna club and beauty salon; but she was not happy there as the salon treated men. Treating men meant harder work, as the main treatment was massage which requires strength from the beauty therapist. In addition, non-members could attend the club, which could be embarrassing as they sometimes misinterpreted the aim of the salon. This made Jo feel uncomfortable. A decision to move south led to a job with an Yves Rocher salon in Maidenhead, where she has been for the last two-and-a-half years.

## Introducing Yvonne

Yvonne Cole is twenty-three years old. She trained as a beauty therapist at the Gloucester College of Arts and started her career with Yves Rocher in Bath, where she improved her speed, gaining good experience by undertaking a wide variety of treatments. She then moved to a large department store in Cheltenham to broaden her experience further, working for a major chain of hairdressing and beauty salons who have many concessions in department stores across the country.

After two years Yvonne felt that she would like to travel and saw an advertisement in one of the major beauty publications, *Beauty Salon*, for work as a beauty therapist on board ship. She decided to apply, and after a rigorous interview she was offered a contract – initially for six months – which she decided to accept. She waited to hear which her first ship would be, and joined it in January 1985.

The company she works for deals with a number of shipping lines: some Italian-owned, some American-owned and some British-owned. They run hairdressing and beauty salons and retail outlets on board. The size of the salons varies enormously depending on the size of the ship; some take one beauty therapist and one hairdresser while others require a whole team of both. The manager/ess of the salons will also manage the retail outlets, which means that they all work as part of the same team, and Yvonne often finds herself sharing accommodation with someone from the retail side.

## Introducing Laura

Twenty-three year-old Laura Rosenbaum trained at the London Institute of Beauty Culture, a private school where she took BABTAC (British Association of Beauty Therapy and Cosmetology) examinations and passed well. Since then she has had three jobs, which she found through local newspaper advertisements. She had rented a flat of her own, but moved back in with her parents when she started up as a mobile therapist. She has set up a beauty room in her parents' house where she treats some clients whilst visiting others. She feels things have gone well during the first ten months, although she says the tax people won't get anything from her this year because her outgoings have been greater than her income: she will not pay any personal tax as her earnings have not reached the minimum threshold. Maybe next year Mr/Mrs Taxperson!

Laura left Coxgreen Comprehensive School with six O-levels and began a secretarial course at a further education college. Having decided after the first year that it was not for her, she went to a private school to train as a beauty therapist. She chose a beauty school in preference to a course at further education college because the latter would have meant waiting until the following September. She enjoyed the course and felt it covered all she needed to do in the job. She hopes to take her CIDESCO (Comité International D'Esthétique et de Cosmétologie) qualification in the next few years. Her ultimate aim is to set up a health hydro.

## Introducing Janine

Janine Hider is twenty-six years old and is at present working for Essanelle based in Dickins & Jones of London. She trained to be a beauty therapist at a further education college, the London College of Fashion, where she took a two-year full-time course leading to City and Guilds examinations. Initially she had hoped to become a make-up artist and had taken a two-year hairdressing course at Tottenham College prior to attending the London College of Fashion. She left school with eight O-levels and so did not have any difficulty obtaining a place at college.

Her first job, which she found by answering an advertisement in the *Hairdressers' Journal*, was with a high street salon in north London. She found the most difficult part of the transition from college to work was the need to sell herself to her clients so that they continued to return to her for treatments. 'Although they teach you to be professional at college, this is something that is hard to grasp until you actually start work.'

After six months Janine decided to set up on her own and pursue her original ambition: concentrating on the make-up side of her work. However, the going was hard and Janine decided to return to full-time employment, taking a job with an Essanelle salon in a Wimbledon department store. Essanelle have moved her around in order to build on her experience, and after a stint in Wood Green she moved to Dickins & Jones. She feels that she is now in the right place to see and experience new things, as Dickins & Jones is an important salon where many new things are tried out by the company.

Janine has recently been made area trainer, which involves her

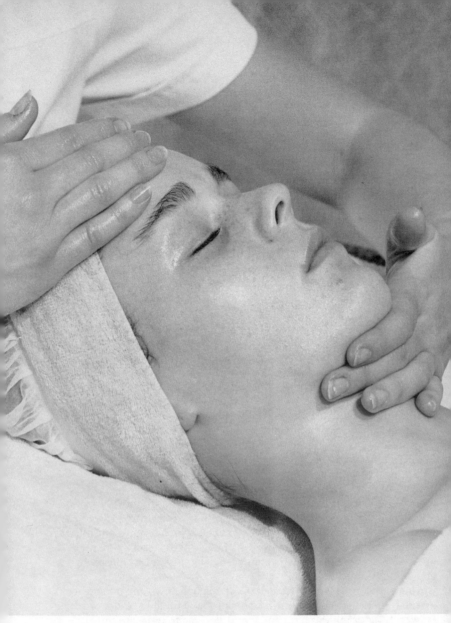

working with beauty therapists new to the company so that they become familiar with the Essanelle way of working. 'We train them to do a full electrolysis consultation with the client; it's important that we maintain the standards that we have built up.'

Janine has recently been sent on a training course by Essanelle in order to learn how to treat red veins, particularly in the facial area. Janine will soon be introducing this treatment at Dickins & Jones.

# 3
## The Treatments

The following is a list of the treatments that are offered by beauty therapists. Not every therapist offers all the treatments; some may specialize in a few or in one. This chapter will give you an outline of some of the main treatments; later chapters will provide more specific details about what they involve.

## Beauty Therapy Treatments

| Facial treatments | Hair removal |
|---|---|
| mini facial, ¾ hour<br>full facial, 1 hour<br>facial with specialist products, 1½ hours<br>eyelash tint<br>eyelash extensions<br>eyebrow shape and/or trim<br>eyebrow tint | *Wax Depilatory*<br>full leg<br>full leg including bikini line<br>half leg<br>full arm<br>underarm<br>forearm<br>facial |
| **Body treatments** | |
| back massage, ½ hour<br>full body massage, 1 hour<br>G5, ½ hour<br>Slendertone (A course of treatments works out cheaper.) | *Creams*<br>bleaching<br>depilatory creams<br><br>*Electrolysis*<br>¼ hour<br>½ hour<br>¾ hour<br>1 hour |
| **Hand and feet treatments** | |
| hand wax treatment, ½ hour<br>manicure<br>pedicure | **Others** |
| **Make-up** | top to toe (facial, body massage, manicure and pedicure), 3 hours |
| cleanse and make-up<br>make-up lesson | |

# Facials

The aim of a facial is to cleanse the skin using creams and oils. The beauty therapist carries out an analysis to decide what treatments are required in order to 'normalize' the skin. The therapist would look for open pores and broken capillaries as well as other conditions which can be affected by the products or treatments available. A course of treatment will then be devised to help the client overcome any problem areas; this may include use of some electrical equipment (see chart entitled 'Electrical Treatments' for more information). Many people attend a salon as a special treat and will not wish to have a course of treatments. The facial can benefit them.

Having removed all traces of make-up from the client's face, the therapist then begins to stimulate the skin by massaging the face, neck and shoulders. A fixed routine is followed, usually lasting twenty minutes, by which time the client should be well relaxed. This will be followed by a face pack mixed, or chosen, to suit the client's skin type. After ten minutes the mask should have done its work of cleansing deeply; it is removed, and the skin is toned and moisturized. A light day make-up is then applied if the client wishes. However, in most cases it is advisable not to indulge in the make-up because it may clog the recently cleansed pores.

Some clients attend a salon regularly for facials, while others have them prior to special occasions. Beauty therapists encourage clients to have a facial about one week before a special occasion because it can sometimes bring impurities in the skin to the surface, which may cause spotting. For those who can afford more regular treatments, a visit to the salon once every two weeks should keep the skin in good order.

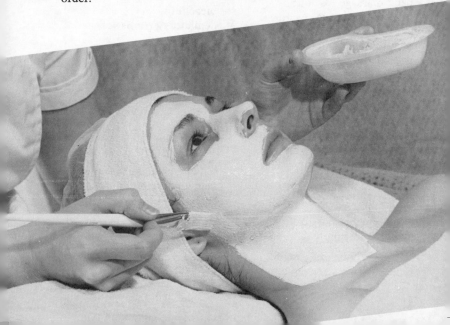

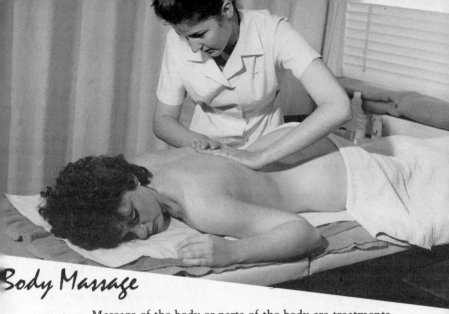

# Body Massage

Massage of the body or parts of the body are treatments that are performed fairly regularly by beauty therapists, and more particularly by masseurs and masseuses. It is usual to find massage offered on a daily basis at health resorts or hydros.

Trainee beauty therapists have to get used to touching every part of the human body. To achieve this they practise doing treatments on each other while they are at college. The big difference between a fellow student and the first client is often size! Trainee beauty therapists are usually people who have always cared for their own bodies, while clients visiting a beauty salon may not have been so disciplined.

Clients normally have a massage in order to help them relax, particularly after a strenuous week. Each area of the body is massaged methodically following a particular routine (which will depend on the technique taught to the therapist during training).

By asking questions about health and by looking for any 'contra-indications' (something which may be harmed by manipulation) prior to starting any treatments, particularly body massage, therapists ensure that they do their clients no harm. High blood pressure may be aggravated if the person with it undergoes a massage. This is one of the treatments where it is essential to have a good understanding of human biology, and it illustrates why most beauty therapy training courses ask for an O-level (or GCSE grade C or above) in a biology-related subject.

Massage can form part of a course of treatments that a client may choose to have. Often electrical treatments will be used with a massage in order to assist the client in losing weight. Beauty therapists offering such treatments would also advise on a suitable calorie-controlled diet with a course of exercise.

| ELECTRICAL TREATMENTS | |
| --- | --- |
| NAME | What it is and how it works |
| *FACIAL TREATMENTS* | |
| VACUUM SUCTION | A glass applicator with variable suction. Helps the circulation of blood and lymph in the skin, revitalizes and rids it of waste. Used to remove blackheads. |
| GALVANIC ROLLERS | Galvanic current (a mild electrical current) passed through rollers to assist the penetration into the skin of creams and oils. A high frequency current creates a tingling feeling. Helps to keep skin germ free. |
| GALVANIC TWEEZERS | Tweezer-like electrodes wrapped in dampened cotton wool. Used to treat greasy skin. |

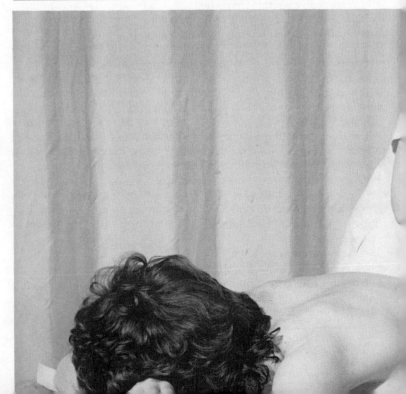

| ELECTRICAL TREATMENTS | |
|---|---|
| NAME | What it is and how it works |
| *BODY TREATMENTS* | |
| GYRATORY VIBRATION MASSAGE | A choice of applicators are available to attach to the gyratory head. Massages parts of the body. Good for spot reducing. |
| VACUUM SUCTION | Large glass applicator with suction used to break down hard fat and release fluid and toxic impurities. A form of automatic massage. |
| FARADIC TREATMENT | Pads applied to areas of muscle which give rhythmical contractions – a form of passive exercise to tone up. |

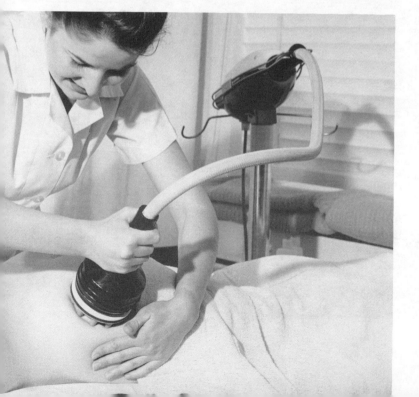

# Make-up

Many people when they talk of beauty therapy assume it is synonymous with make-up. They assume that beauty therapists spend most of their day applying, and advising customers on, make-up products. In fact, this is only a small part of a beauty therapist's job and plays only a very minor role in the syllabus of any beauty therapy training course. Clients that do attend a salon for make-up do so to learn how to make themselves up or to be professionally made up for a special event in their lives.

Many brides-to-be discuss make-up ideas for the big day with a beauty therapist at the local beauty salon. These are known as 'make-up lessons', and involve the therapist talking through with the client the effect she would like and then demonstrating on the client the best way to achieve this.

Make-up lessons are not always for brides. Other clients include those who may have a facial blemish that they would like camouflaged. This could be anything from inset eyes to strawberry birthmarks. The more serious cases require slightly different techniques and sometimes specialist products. Most courses teach 'cosmetic

camouflage' and emphasize the importance of personal tact as well as the more technical skills of skin analysis. An understanding of cosmetic science will also be necessary in order that no products are used which might aggravate the problem.

Some clients prefer not to learn the techniques themselves but would rather the beauty therapist made them up for those special occasions. Sadly, these clients are few and far between, much to the dismay of most therapists who like the opportunity to exercise their artistic abilities. 'Fantasy make-up' skills, which really require artistic skill, are taught on most further education college courses. Students learn how to produce special effects on the face and/or body: birds flying around the model's neck, or models' bodies painted to look like animals, perhaps a tiger. Unfortunately these skills are rarely employed by the majority of qualified beauty therapists, certainly not by those employed in high street beauty salons. Those therapists who master the skills and who can find a model who will sit still for hours of practice, sometimes enter national and international competitions, which give them the opportunity to indulge themselves. To find out about the work of the make-up artist, look at the chapter in Part Two of this book (see p. 94).

# Hair Removal: Waxing

The removal of unwanted hair is the most common treatment offered by high street beauty salons and department store salons. The removal of hair can take various forms.

Waxing is a method of temporarily removing unwanted hair. It is a very popular treatment and one which clients who do not attend a beauty salon on a regular basis will undergo. It is particularly popular during the summer months as clients prepare themselves for their beach holidays.

There are two methods of waxing available to a therapist. The decision as to which is the most appropriate is based either on a particular client's need or on the therapist's preference. The two waxes are known as 'hot wax' and 'strip wax'. The latter is more widely used as it tends to be less messy.

The hot wax method involves applying a hot thick wax with a wooden spatula (some salons use a wooden kitchen spoon) to the area from which the hair must be removed. Once the wax becomes cool – but not too brittle – the therapist quickly rips the wax off in the opposite direction to the hair growth. This removes the hairs from the

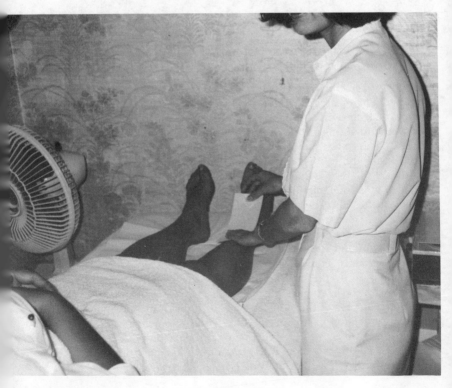

roots. It has been likened to the feeling of pulling off a plaster from a hairy part of the body! In fact it is not as painful as it sounds, and becomes even less so after the first few treatments. Many people feel that the short- and long-term benefits outweigh the short period of discomfort.

The strip wax method is not unlike the hot wax: both have the same effect. The wax in this method is much thinner and can be applied at a much cooler temperature with a smaller spatula. The area covered by each strip tends to be smaller, which allows this method to be used on areas like the upper lip or eyebrow. Once the wax has been applied, a piece of material or waxed paper is placed on top and the whole quickly ripped off in the same way as in the hot wax method.

People have a number of areas of their bodies waxed to remove unwanted hair. The most common area for women is the lower leg and bikini line. In comparison to shaving the hair away, this method is superior because it leaves the area feeling smoother and the hair takes much longer to grow back, usually four to six weeks depending on the hair's strength and density. Those who regularly have their legs waxed find that the hair becomes finer and tends to thin out.

# Hair Removal: Electrolysis

This is said to be the only safe and permanent way of removing unwanted hair. Many areas of the body can be treated in order to remove hair; the most common problem is unwanted hair on the face, which often occurs in women on the chin or upper lip. However the hands, legs, stomach and chest are also treated on a regular basis, depending on the needs of the individual client.

The presence of unwanted hair can have a traumatic effect on some clients; the therapist must be tactful and sympathetic. The treatment involves inserting a needle into each hair follicle; the therapist uses a magnifying glass and works under a strong light in order to do this effectively. The therapist then sends an electric current into the needle which has the effect of cauterizing the follicle and preventing further hair growth. The therapist calculates the strength of the current required to be effective. The hair may cease to grow immediately, but it is more likely that each hair follicle will have to be treated a number of times. The length of treatment will depend on the strength of the hair. Appointments last between ten and thirty minutes and may be held once a week over a two-year period. Naturally the length of treatment will depend on a number of factors, not least the area of the hair to be removed.

Clients vary in their reaction to the treatment. Some find it quite painful at first, others experience a tingling sensation running down their spine during the treatment. It is essential that those interested in

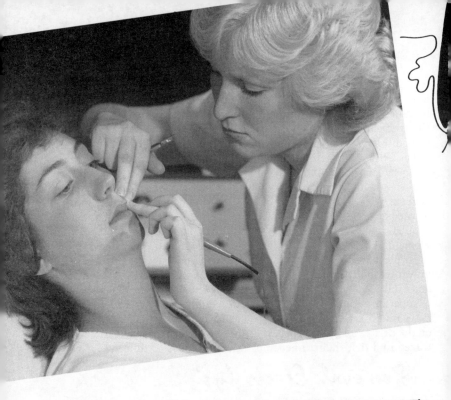

undergoing a period of treatment visit a qualified practitioner. The equipment can cause burning or even permanent scarring if misused.

A practised therapist should be able to put the clients at their ease and explain the treatment fully. The therapist should be tactful and very patient. All beauty salons now offer electrolysis as a treatment; in many cases it is the most popular treatment available.

### Janine comments on doing electrolysis

I enjoy doing electrolysis because I feel I'm achieving something for my client; I can actually see definite results both at the end of each appointment and at the end of a course of treatment. Some people find that they have to attend a salon more regularly than others because the hormonal make-up of each body is different. This affects the strength of the hair, and the stronger the hair the longer the period of time before the treatment is effective. I suppose there are people for whom electrolysis doesn't work, but I have never met any.

I see most of my clients for quarter of an hour once a week for the first six months to a year; after that it may be less often, perhaps once a month. The relationship can be for as long as two years, in some cases more, depending on what part of the body I am working on. It's nice to get to know your clients in this way because both the client and I feel more relaxed in each other's company.

I mainly treat facial hair as this is the area where most people find unwanted hair causes most embarrassment. I have to start with the electrical current really low and work up, so that I can take the hair out without tugging at it but also not scar the skin with too much heat. Eventually finding the mid-point becomes easy; often I can just tell by looking at the hair: the stronger the hair the higher the current.

I have had a few clients who have ceased to have electrolysis since AIDS became a big issue. We have always used disposable needles and we use a needle for each client. I do my best to reassure the clients that our methods are very safe and hygienic.

Recent training to extend my work as a electrologist in the salon has meant that I now have the British Medical Aesthetic Association Certificate to show that I can do red vein treatment. The method is very similar to that of electrolysis, in that a needle is inserted into the facial capillary and the electrical current then cauterizes it, thereby preventing the blood returning to the area. This is more expensive than electrolysis because a client will only have one capillary done once, while a hair follicle may have to be treated four or five times.

Good eyesight and lots of patience are the main skills required to do electrolysis all day and every day. It's a very methodical treatment.

## The most popular treatments

Salons do vary in their reports on the treatment in greatest demand. Obviously there is a seasonal variation which makes beauty salons more popular during the summer months. Each salon will vary its list of treatments available according to the type of client group it is dealing with. In general health resorts tend to offer more body treatments, while high street salons offer treatments like electrolysis which require a more regular attendance pattern.

The most common treatments are:

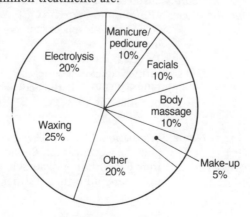

# 4
## How do Beauty Therapists Train?

COLLEGE COURSES

*Name*: City and Guilds 302–305
*Length of Course*: 2 years full-time
*Exam Board*: City and Guilds of London Institute
*Entry Qualifications*: *Minimum Preferred* 3 GCSEs grade C or above or 3 O-levels or equivalent, to include Biology
*Age*: 16 years or over
*Found at*: further education colleges

*Name*: BTEC (or SCOTVEC) National Diploma in Beauty Therapy
*Length of Course*: 2 years full-time
*Exam Board*: Business and Technician Education Council
*Entry Qualifications*: *Minimum Preferred* 4 GCSEs grade C or above or 4 O-levels or equivalent, to include Biology
*Age*: 16 years or over
*Found at*: further education colleges

*Name*: BTEC (or SCOTVEC) Higher National Diploma in Beauty Therapy
*Length of Course*: 2 years full-time
*Exam Board*: Business and Technician Education council
*Entry Qualifications*: *Minimum Preferred* 2 GCE A-levels plus GCSEs or O-levels or equivalent to include Biology
*Age*: 18 years or over
*Found at*: further education colleges
NB: SCOTVEC is the Scottish equivalent qualification to BTEC.

*Name*: International Beauty Therapists Diploma plus the Certificate in Epilation
*Length of Course*: from 6 months in private schools (full-time) to 2 years full-time at further education colleges

*Exam Board*: International Health and Beauty Council (IHBC)
*Entry Qualifications*: *Minimum Preferred* 4 GCSEs grade C or above or 4 O-levels or equivalent, to include Biology
*Age*: 16 or over
*Found at*: further education colleges and private beauty schools

*Name*: British Association of Beauty Therapy and Cosmetology (BABTAC)
*Length of Course*: from 6 months to 12 months full-time Students whose pass mark exceeds 70 per cent are eligible to undertake the CIDESCO examination on courses of more than 10 months in length (the Comité International D'Esthétique et de Cosmétologie).
*Exam Board*: Confederation of International Beauty Therapy and Cosmetology (CIBTAC)
*Entry Qualifications*: *Minimum Preferred*: 3 GCSEs grade C or above or 3 O-levels or equivalent, to include English and a science subject
*Age*: 17 ½ when sitting the examination
*Found at*: private schools or further education colleges

*Name*: ITEC Beauty Therapy Diploma and Electrology Certificate
*Length of Course*: from 6 months full-time to 2 years full-time
*Exam Board*: International Therapy Examination Council
*Entry Qualifications*: *Minimum Preferred* 5 GCSEs grade C or above or 5 O-levels or equivalent, to including English. Entrants over 30 years at the discretion of the Principal.
*Age*: 16 or over
*Found at*: private schools or further education colleges

31

There are three main ways that beauty therapists can train:

# Full-time College Course

The most popular method of training is by attending a full-time college course. Courses exist at further education colleges run by Local Education Authorities and at private schools of beauty. Both can offer recognized qualifications, but often their training methods are different. Further education college courses invariably last for two years (if they specialize in beauty), while those offered by private schools are more concentrated and can be as short as six months. The course syllabus usually dictates the minimum number of hours that should be devoted to a particular topic. It is then up to the school or college to decide how much time is allowed for each topic and when it is covered. Private schools often insist that students attend classes/lectures in the evenings and expect the students to undertake additional private study, thereby shortening the length of the course. In addition, it is unlikely that students will be allowed holidays during their time with the school (public holidays excepted, of course).

Private schools are not able to offer courses with qualifications awarded by the City and Guilds of London Institute or the Business and Technician Education Council, or their Scottish equivalent (see College Courses chart, pp. 30, 31). These examination bodies also make awards in other professional areas, therefore employers outside the beauty industry recognize holders as having reached a specific academic standard. The other examination bodies mentioned in the chart are peculiar to the beauty industry; along with City and Guilds and BTEC they are equally acceptable to the employers in the industry, but may not be accepted by employers outside the industry. This is worth bearing in mind if you feel you may wish to change careers later on.

The College Course chart shows the qualifications and courses that are available and where they may be found. These are the only recognized examinations. Some private schools of beauty offer their own diplomas, but these may not (probably will not) be recognized by all employers in the beauty industry. If you decide to apply to a private school, ensure that they offer all the items on the Private Schools Checklist at the end of this chapter (see p. 39).

Many of the examination boards offer modular study packages, which means you can take part of the course and sit an examination in it. For example, you could take the manicure module and sit an examination, which would allow you (if you pass) to do a job only as a manicurist. If you wish to be a fully qualified beauty therapist or aestheticienne and electrologist (this term is sometimes used to

| Examining bodies | Components required |
| --- | --- |
| City and Guilds of London Institute | Beauty Therapist Certificate 304<br>Electrical Epilation Certificate 305 |
| Confederation of International Beauty Therapy and Cosmetology | Beauticians Diploma<br>Body Therapist<br>Electrolysist Diploma |
| International Health and Beauty Council | The International Beauty Therapist Diploma<br>The Certificate in Epilation |
| Business and Technician Education Council (BTEC) | BTEC National Diploma in Beauty Therapy |
| International Therapy Examination Council | Beauty Therapy Diploma (Part A Beauty; Part B Therapy)<br>Electrology Certificate |

describe the job of a beauty therapist), it is essential to undertake study and examinations in all areas of the syllabus.

The chart above shows which examinations you must sit with which board to be a fully qualified beauty therapist – naturally you have to pass the examinations to qualify. The pass mark varies according to the examination board. Some offer credits and distinctions if you get a very good mark. Confederation schools offer opportunity to students to continue to study for the CIDESCO qualification if they achieve a pass mark of more than 70 per cent, This is one of the qualifications that has international recognition.

Some colleges offer hairdressing and beauty courses combined. These courses normally last for three years and are only run by further education colleges. In most cases the examinations on the hairdressing side lead to a City and Guilds qualification. However, the award on the beauty side may be from any one of the examination bodies listed. On some combined courses there is not enough time available to train students to be full beauty therapist. Therefore the qualification you would obtain would only allow you to practise as a beautician (see the chapter on the role of the beautician for further details). This is often why courses offering both hairdressing and beauty do not ask for as many entry qualifications as do the courses training you to be a beauty therapist. To make sure you are being trained in the areas that you wish, find out whether *all* the examinations listed for the relevant examining body are being offered.

Some of the courses offered can be studied on a part-time basis in the evening or at weekends. This is particularly true of private schools in the London area where demand for this method of study is high, especially from more mature entrants. Obviously training can take a long time, but it allows people to work during the day.

## The syllabuses

All the courses mentioned cover the main treatments and subjects required to be a beauty therapist. Further education colleges have more time to cover the subjects in greater depth. They also have the opportunity to offer additional subjects like design or psychology. Students attending these courses may find they have a stronger position in the employment market. It is possible to find alternative therapies on the agenda at both further education colleges and private schools. The latter would make a higher charge for additional subjects.

Write to the examination boards to find out the differences in the syllabus (the addresses are at the end of this chapter, see pp. 42, 43) or arrange a visit to your local beauty training establishments to compare the courses, before deciding on the most appropriate course for you.

### The Essential Subjects to Look For

Manicure. Pedicure. Make-up (day and evening). Corrective make-up. Photographic make-up. Eyebrow shaping. Eyelash treatments (tinting and extensions). Facial treatments (face masks, specialized facial treatments, rehydration, muscle tone and massage). Superfluous hair removal (hot and strip waxing, bleaching, creams). Body massage (figure analysis). Treatments involving electrical equipment (vacuum suction, gyratory massage, faradism, galvanism, infra-red radiant heat, ultra-violet). Steam, foam, sauna and paraffin wax baths. Electrolysis.

### Other Subjects to Look For

Professional ethics (reception of clientele, tact, diplomacy, communication between client and therapist). Equipment care, selection, health and safety aspects, sterilization. Diet and nutrition. Exercise, deportment and balance. Salon organization. Science (human biology, physical science, cosmetic chemistry). First aid. Communication studies. Physics. Chemistry. Biology. Business studies.

## What form does the teaching take?

All courses offer a combination of practical and theoretical sessions. During the practical sessions students have to be prepared to undergo all the treatments offered by beauty therapists. This is because it is essential for therapists to talk knowledgeably to their clients about the effect a treatment will have and how it will feel. Knowing how a treatment really feels not only allows therapists to talk sensibly about it, but also helps them sell treatments to their clients.

Selling, although not on the syllabus, is a very significant part of a beauty therapist's job. Not only will they sell additional treatments to clients, they will also sell products. Most salons promote a particular product range: the staff use it during treatments and recommend it to their clients to use on a regular basis. This can be a major source of additional income for the salon owner and also for the therapist, who may earn commission. Another very important reason for students to act as models for their classmates is that it would be difficult to get models to volunteer while a therapist is in the initial stages of training. Plenty will appear for free or relatively cheap treatments when the students are fairly proficient at their art, but there are few people prepared to endure the pain of a student's first go at waxing! Initial mistakes have to be made on fellow trainees!

## Examinations

The examinations take a similar form to the teaching, in that they are a combination of practical work and written theory. The practical examinations involve being monitored by the examiner while treating a model. Both facial and body treatments are examined by this method, along with waxing and electrolysis. The number of examinations will depend on the examination board; on average two practical sessions cover the subjects mentioned above. Each practical exam lasts for about two hours. BTEC does not have exams, relying instead on continual assessment of the course work. City and Guilds includes an element of continual assessment, some of the marks from the course work undertaken during the two years going towards the final result.

## Who pays?

*For further education college study*
Students under eighteen years of age will normally have their fees paid by their Local Education Authority if they are attending a course in the area covered by the Authority. If no course is offered within their boundaries, the Authority will pay for students to attend courses offered by other Authorities. It is worth obtaining a list of courses that the Authority will sponsor before making your application.

The Government is currently reassessing the way Local Authorities fund students on courses. It may be possible in the future to choose the college you wish to attend and be sponsored on it even if there is a course closer to your home. Travel expenses may also be covered if a student lives beyond a specified distance from the college. However, additional costs like uniforms, some textbooks and equipment may have to be borne by the student and his or her parents or guardian. This is in addition to living costs for which a grant is not usually

Students in training at
Champneys College
of Health and Beauty.

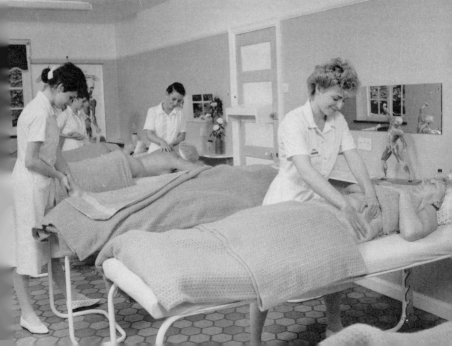

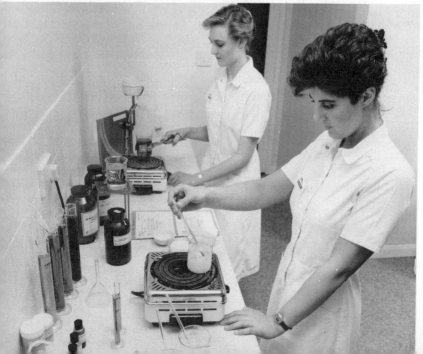

obtainable. For those over eighteen years of age it is worth researching into discretionary awards made by some Local Education Authorities.

The BTEC Higher National Diploma course is post A-level and therefore only accepts students who are over eighteen years of age. It is therefore possible to get a mandatory award from the Local Education Authority which pays the fees and helps towards living expenses. It is important to check with your Local Education Authority before assuming that you are entitled to a grant.

*For private schools*
Courses offered by private schools can work out extremely expensive, as students not only have to find course fees but also have to support themselves. The actual cost will vary according to location. London-based courses are the most expensive, although London does boast some of the better-known schools. The cost of most full-time private courses starts at £1,500. The fee may include the provision of textbooks and the use of salon equipment; however these are areas to check out at the interview when you can discuss what you get for your money. Private courses are not sponsored by Local Education Authorities or any other organizations. Occasionally, when no suitable course is run within travelling distance, an LEA may offer financial assistance, but this is very rare. Some charitable organizations have been known to help particular students in need, but they are few and far between.

**Checklist of things to find out when applying to a further education college course**

**1.** Will you be taking enough modules to make you a fully qualified beauty therapist? Are all facial and body treatments covered? Will you be trained to do electrolysis? (This is especially worth remembering if the course is combined with hairdressing or is only offered to young people who have completed a hairdressing course.)

**2.** Are you eligible to have your fees paid?

**3.** What are the additional costs, for example books, uniforms, tuition for alternative therapies?

**Joanne comments on attending a further education college**

I felt that the course was very worthwhile – I learnt a lot. I don't know how some people coped with the academic side of the course without a high standard of Biology behind them; my Biology A-level was invaluable to me.

We covered a lot of subjects outside beauty therapy which were very useful. Some have already been helpful and others I think will help me in the future. The business studies element was very strong. We had to do a project on setting up a beauty salon within a specified budget. We contacted manufacturers, even chose the wallpaper that we would put up. The experience will be useful to me as I plan to start up my own business eventually, once I have got the money. I think I will have to move up north again to do this, because accommodation and business premises costs in this area are exorbitant and the wages are no higher.

### Janine comments on attending a further education college

I went to a further education college to do City and Guilds qualifications in beauty therapy (before BTEC had become involved in awarding qualifications). I had the right entry qualifications and felt I wanted to learn as much as I could about the job I was going into so as to be able to do it really well.

I felt that the course was very good and that at the end of it I was ready to start work. I didn't find the speed a problem when I did start work because all the practical examinations I had sat had strict time limits which ensured that I built up my speed. However, I did find that after some time in the job my speed improved, particularly on the waxing, to the point where I was finishing well within the allotted time which gave me more time to prepare for the next client.

The theory element of the course was very important and I don't think you can ever have enough; that's why I took, and passed, a Human Biology A-level in evening classes this year. You get asked all sorts of questions in the salon by clients, to which they expect an answer; some can be really technical. A good and accurate answer is essential – after all, you are doing all sorts of things to their bodies and they have a right to know whether there is any danger. I have to say I have had clients who have been treated by beauty therapists elsewhere and who have been told a range of strange things bearing no relation to what was really happening. It is better to say 'I don't know' than to make up answers.

### Checklist of things to find out when applying to private schools

**1.** Is the school offering examinations leading to a recognized qualification? (Some schools say they study a particular syllabus but do not actually have links with the examination board and are therefore not able to enter you for the examination.)
**2.** Does the training lead to you becoming a fully qualified beauty

therapist? (The syllabus should cover electrical treatments including electrolysis.)

**3.** Does the fee cover books, equipment, uniforms and examination entry fees? Are there any additional charges for particular areas of the syllabus?

**4.** What happens if you fail one of the examinations? Do you pay for extra tuition? Does entering the examination again cost more?

# Working Pupil

This is another method of training to be a beauty therapist. It has now become quite difficult to find salons that are prepared to take on this kind of traineee. Trainees pay a fee to a qualified beauty therapist who then allows the traineee to work alongside, watching and learning at the same time. The therapist has to make time to teach the theoretical aspects of the syllabus. If you are interested in this method of training you will need to be very well motivated as you will have to do a lot of private study after your working day is finished.

The length of training will vary according to the salon offering it; it can take between one and two years. As a trainee you are involved in other duties in the salon like reception work and clearing up at the end of the day. ITEC is one of the examination boards that produces a list of tutors who are prepared to offer training in this way. At the end of the designated period you attend an examination centre where you are examined along with other working pupils, possibly at a school near you that is examining it own students. It is more likely, however, that you would have to travel to a major city to sit the exam. The examinations are often held in London.

There are both advantages and disadvantages to being a working pupil. On the one hand, as the only trainee you receive all the trainer's attention. On the other, the trainer might have a rush of clients, leaving you very much the observer. In addition, finding models to practise upon may prove difficult. It would not be possible for you to work on paying clients, so you may spend a lot of time convincing your family and friends that you are ready to treat them!

**Checklist of things to find out when applying to be a working pupil**

**1.** Does the training cover all aspects of beauty therapy?

**2.** What examination board does the syllabus follow? Is it a recognized one?

**3.** Is there a set period for the training to last?

**4.** Will you follow a structured training programme so that you know roughly what topics you will be covering on which days?

**5.** How will you get your practice?

**6.** Where will you take your examinations?

**7.** How much will the training cost you? Does this include textbooks, equipment and examination entry fees?

# Apprenticeship

This is the final method of training to be a beauty therapist. It is the least common of the methods outlined. It operates in a similar way to a hairdressing apprenticeship. A beauty salon may employ a junior to do all the menial tasks like salon preparation, cleaning, reception and general assistant duties. The training element of the apprenticeship would take place between appointments and at specified times during the week.

The training could last for as long as three years; the length of time depends very much on how determined the salon is to get you through to the final examination. The most successful apprenticeships are those which offer some form of indentureship, ensuring that the salon states at the beginning of the training period exactly how long it will last and what will be covered. This form of contract is then binding on both employer and employee.

Fortunately very few salons now offer this form of training. In the past employers took on young people with few qualifications and kept them working as assistants, never allowing them the time to qualify as beauty therapists.

**Checklist of things to find out when applying to be an apprenticed beauty therapist**

**1.** Are you going to be given a contract outlining the training covered and a set timescale for it?

**2.** Is the salon offering a set syllabus leading to a recognized qualification?

3. Will you have to pay for the examinations entrance fee? Where will the examinations be held?

**4.** How many other people have the salon trained in this way and how successful were they?

**5.** What will your wages be and how often will you get a rise?

# YTS

The Training Commission runs a scheme designed to assist young people leaving school or college to train in their chosen careers. You may be entitled to a place on the scheme for one or two years if you meet the eligibility criteria. Your local Careers Office or Jobcentre will have details of any managing agents offering beauty training in your area and will be able to tell you whether you are eligible to join.

Those schemes offering beautician and beauty therapy training find you a work-experience placement with a beauty salon. You undertake similar tasks to an apprenticed beautician or beauty therapist. During your first year you are entitled to thirteen weeks off-the-job training (seven weeks in your second year) and will probably be given day or block release to a local college or beauty school. You will also cover subjects like communication skills and computer literacy.

You will receive a small training allowance, and will get a YTS certificate and a recognized qualification at the end of your course.

**Checklist of the things to find out when applying to a YTS programme**

**1.** Are you going to cover all the skills required to be a fully qualified beauty therapist? (If the scheme is going to train you as a beautician, read the chapter 'Beauticians', p. 75.)

**2.** Is the scheme offering a set syllabus leading to a recognized beauty qualification which will allow you to practise as a beautician or beauty therapist if you pass the examinations?

**3.** What opportunities are open to you at the end of the training scheme?

**Where to find out more**

For information on the availability of courses in your area and an opportunity to examine the variety of syllabuses, write to:

The City and Guilds of London Institute
Section 24
46 Britannia Street
London WC1X 9RG

The Business and Technician Education Council (BTEC)
Information Service
Central House
Upper Woburn Place
London WC1H 0HH

The Scottish Vocational Education Council (SCOTVEC)
22 Great King Street
Edinburgh EH3 6QH
*or*
38 Queen Street
Glasgow G1 3DY

The British Association of Beauty Therapy and Cosmetology Ltd
CIBTAC Secretariat
Suite 5, Wolseley House
Oriel Road
Cheltenham
Gloucestershire GL50 1TH

The International Health and Beauty Council
109A Felpham Road
Felpham
West Sussex PO22 7PW

International Therapy Education Council
Secretariat
16 Avenue Place
Harrogate
North Yorkshire HG2 7PJ

# 5

## Where do Beauty Therapists Work?

## High Street Salon

High street salons are where most beauty therapists work. This has become the case particularly in latter years because so many new salons have opened up to meet increased demand from the public. There is a growing awareness of the need to be fit and look good, but Britain has, in fact, only recently begun to catch up in this area with its European counterparts, who have always shown great interest in health and beauty. This is especially true of France. Nowadays, though, most towns in Britain boast at least one beauty salon.

A typical salon will employ three or four beauty therapists and a receptionist; the owner often working in the salon. Most beauty course leavers find their initial employment in high street salons. It is particularly hard at first because the new recruit is kept busy with an almost unending list of clients. Further education college leavers who begin their working life just before the summer rush find themselves thrown in at the deep end! Your main problem may well be lack of speed, and time is money! In addition you will see one client after another, which may not have happened during a college day. Therefore stamina is very important; lunch breaks are rarely regular and often have to be snatched between appointments.

You begin by building up your client group; you need to be good otherwise your clients will not come back to you. You must therefore keep smiling through the strain. Money should not be a key motivating factor for you because you will not earn a lot at the beginning. But never fear – things do improve! As your client group grows you may begin to earn commission on the work you are doing and on the product sales you are making. Of course, tips are always an added bonus.

The main treatments you will undertake are those to do with hair removal, and it will not be long before you are really fast at waxing. A beauty salon in a high street is often a good place to get your initial experience because therapists here do not specialize too early. It is possible that other establishments would expect you to concentrate on one type of treatment. This is fine later on in your career but restricting if you do so too early.

The hours can be a little anti-social because you will work most Saturdays – this is usually the salon's busiest day – and at least one late evening each week. In addition to your duties as a beauty therapist you may also be expected to act as a receptionist between appointments, make tea and coffee for your clients, prepare your treatment area and clear up after yourself ready for the next day. The frequency of these duties will depend on the size of the salon and its location.

### Joanne comments on working in a high street salon

There are three beauty therapists in addition to myself. We also have a part-time receptionist to help on busy days, as well as the owner who no longer treats clients but does help out on reception. We are very busy at the moment because, being summer, it is peak time and we have just had two new beauty therapists join us straight from college. That means I have had to take on some extra responsibility until they get settled, and then we will share it between us.

I chose to work in a high street salon because I like the variety of treatments; I think working on a health farm would involve me in too much body work, which is OK but not all the time. I spent some time working in a hotel, which in some ways was not much different as I had some regular clients from the local area as well as hotel guests. However the number of regular clients was outweighed by guests; I suppose the mixture will depend very much on how many beauty salons there are in the area. I didn't really like being regularly confronted with strangers.

It's nice to build up a regular clientele and get to know them. I think it's lucky that I have a good memory because you really get to know people's problems and it's essential if they tell you something that you remember it the next time you see them, otherwise they are very hurt. Occasionally I have resorted to writing a few notes on a client's record card when I have been told something which it is pertinent to recall. For example, one of my clients had a nervous breakdown and I didn't want to put my foot in it after a gap between appointments.

Electrolysis and waxing are the two treatments that I do most often. I enjoy both of them as I can see a result fairly quickly and that is satisfying for me. I'm not too keen on the treatments involving a lot of physical work like G5 and massage. Not only do they involve a lot of hard work but it is not always possible to see any benefit, although obviously the client will feel benefits. G5 normally consists of a six-week course, so if you can remember what the client looked like in the beginning then you may gain some satisfaction. Fortunately I don't have to do these treatments very often. I suppose the second area that I treat regularly is the face, usually eyelash tinting and eyebrow trims.

The salon receives a lot of letters from people wanting to go into beauty therapy. Some already have been on courses, others want advice on how to train. Some people have partially trained and specialized in one specific area of the work. They are no good in a high street salon because you need to be able to do every treatment to be useful. I think the biggest disadvantage of this job is the money – that's my only regret: it's so low. The basic is the same irrespective of the part of the country that you're living in. The only way to earn more is to work harder to increase the commission you receive on sales. Otherwise I still have to say that I enjoy what I do because it gives me a lot of variety.

'

## Department Store

Many major department stores have beauty salons attached to their hairdressing salons. They are normally run by a company that has the concession for this operation. Essanelle, for example, have a number of salons in major department stores throughout the country as well as some free-standing hairdressing salons.

The work in each store varies according to its location. Some act as the local beauty salon, operating like high street salons, and offer the same treatments. Others, particularly those based in major towns or cities, tend to offer more specialist treatments in addition to those offered by the beauty therapist. It is common to find a masseuse, a nail technician, an electrologist and even some alternative therapists working in major department stores.

Department stores prefer to take on experienced beauty therapists, as their clients have high expectations of the quality of service they should receive. The client group will vary depending on the location; stores in London and other major cities find that they offer treatments to many working women in both executive and routine jobs. Other clients include tourists and one or two local people living in up-market areas of the city. The age range is from eighteen to eighty, although the majority fall in the middle. The wide age group is because the major treatment that the salons do is electrolysis. Unwanted hair, particularly on the face, can affect any age group.

The salons' busiest times are during lunchtimes and after work. Saturdays are not as busy because many of the client group are in Monday to Friday jobs. There are also busy times of the year, which will depend on the most popular treatments used in the salons. In the case of the Essanelle salon in Dickins & Jones of London, the most popular treatments are electrolysis and waxing, and the busiest time is therefore the summer. The salon is quieter after Christmas, probably because most of the client group spent their money on Christmas presents! In addition, they are probably visiting the sales and spending next month's salary, too.

There are advantages in working for a major company, especially for a salon based in a department store. Most have a reputation to maintain and will have up-to-date equipment and a pleasant working environment. Larger companies will often send their staff on updating courses or have them trained in new techniques in order to offer their client group the most modern methods of treatment. On a more practical level, the therapist enjoys all the advantages of working in a department store: subsidized food in the staff canteen, discount on purchases within the store and so on. The hours will be the same as those worked by store staff, so although Saturdays will be obligatory there will only be one late night a week.

### Janine comments on working in a department store

Much of my time is devoted to doing electrolysis, which happened initially because I replaced an Electrologist who had been doing only that. Added to this I brought some of my clients with me from Wood Green, which was OK because I was working for the same company. If I hadn't been I would have been in trouble, because in most salons you have to sign a 'radius clause' which means you can't take a job within a certain area of the salon; the idea is to prevent you stealing clients.

I'd say 70 per cent of my time is devoted to electrolysis now, which is not uncommon in a beauty salon. It has always been the treatment that I have done most wherever I have worked. After electrolysis I find myself doing waxing most and then facials, eyebrow trims and eyelash tints. I expect the variety of treatments a beauty therapist would get to do would depend on the store. If there is someone employed to do only electrolysis the beauty therapist would end up doing mainly waxing and facials. Some salons have specific accommodation available for a masseuse, with a shower room attached to the cubicle. In those cases a therapist would find that they would do very little body massage – only when the masseuse was fully booked.

I have recently been trained to do red vein treatment and we are beginning this in the salon. Since I'm the only one trained, if it takes off I'll probably spend a lot of time doing this. I have a regular clientele which I have built up, and most days I find myself fully booked. It's a job where you have to be patient all the time, very flexible, there is no point in getting moody or uptight. Being professional is really the most important aspect. All day long you're hurting people and you need to be able to cope with that and to help your clients cope. You have to treat them all as individuals and help them to relax. You need to look the part, not over made-up – the clients prefer the clinical look because in most cases they treat you like a nurse or a doctor. They will ask you about other problems they may have; you have got to know when to refer them to their doctor, to know when you have reached the limit of your knowledge.

# Health Farm

This was traditionally where the general public thought all beauty therapists were employed. They were seen as something that only the rich could enjoy, and therefore as something rather decadent and unnecessary. However times have changed and it has become much more acceptable to have beauty treatments and to look after one's body. The picture of health farms or resorts as places where the clients are locked in for a week in order drastically to lose weight is now old-fashioned. Opportunities for dieting are available, but the emphasis is on helping clients relax away from the stress of day-to-day living.

Health farms offer treatments beyond those offered by beauty

Champneys Health Resort at Tring.

therapists. They employ a variety of specialists, among whom there is a place for the beauty therapist. These include masseurs or masseuses, aerobics teachers, osteopaths and dieticians, among others. Some farms offer access to a resident doctor or to one on call to give advice to clients or to serve their health needs. This would depend very much on the size of the establishment.

Because the beauty element of the treatments on offer is only a small part of the work of the farm, there are few vacancies available for beauty therapists. It is, however, the environment in which many would wish to work. It can be a very stimulating environment because of the variety of skills possessed by one's colleagues.

Health farms tend to employ more experienced therapists because of the nature of the client group. The preference is for therapists who have two or more years' work experience before joining the staff team. The work is different from the traditional beauty salon as certain treatments are emphasized. You will probably find yourself offering more facials and spending more time looking after the sunbed and sauna clients than elsewhere. Massage, exercise and dietetics are the responsibility of other specialists.

Most health farms are located in beautiful countryside in buildings with plenty of character. The facilities are usually excellent, with swimming pools, jacuzzis, tennis courts and other sporting facilities as well as spacious beauty salons with very up-to-date equipment, which altogether offer therapists a luxurious working environment. The disadvantage in the location is that it is often necessary to live in, which is not acceptable to some. On the other hand, staff are generally allowed to use the facilities at off-peak times.

## Alison comments on working on a health farm

I worked at a health resort for one-and-a-half years. I began by living in the resort as it was quite a distance from my home. Then the resort bought a house five or six miles away into which two

The swimming pool at Champneys.

other therapists and I moved. After a time I found I missed my social life at home, particularly my boyfriend and my family, so I moved home again and commuted to work by car.

Initially I worked a fairly regular day. However, the resort found that the clients were becoming bored in the evenings so they decided that beauty treatments should be available then. The plan was to increase the number of beauty treatments sold, since under the old system the clients were often busy during the day with exercise. Of course we then had to begin working a shift system, which involved us in more evening and weekend work. This also had a bad effect on my social life.

I enjoyed the variety of work at the health resort and the environment was super, as were the clients and staff. But I found it frustrating that I could not build up a regular clientele. I was seeing different faces each week and I never knew whether clients really liked the treatments I gave them. The only way of knowing that is if a client comes back to you for another appointment, and at a health resort, particularly on a shift system, clients could rarely do that even if they wanted to.

I would say it would be good experience for a therapist to work at a health resort because of the facilities. However it is difficult to get promotion, as the senior positions are occupied for a long time. The responsibility that any individual therapist could take on is limited. I felt ready to take on more responsibility and so decided to move on. I also wanted to earn more, which is quite difficult in the beauty business as most places pay poorly, but most health resorts only pay commission on product sales over a target figure. This is fairly easily reached but it doesn't make you rich.

# On Board Ship

This is the environment in which many aspiring beauty therapists wish to work because it conjures up pictures of a glamorous life on the ocean waves! Although opportunities do exist they are not as common as beauty therapists would hope; therefore competition to obtain the jobs that are available is very strong.

Most major cruise liners have a hairdressing and beauty salon combined – employing both hairdressers and beauty therapists – as part of the service that they offer to their passengers. These salons are usually offered as concessions to large hairdressing and beauty organizations.

Such companies have very high standards when recruiting staff to work on board the ships. They look for a maturity which they feel recently qualified beauty therapists lack. They often stipulate that applicants should be over twenty years of age with at least two years' experience of working as a beauty therapist. Even suitably qualified therapists who meet these criteria are frequently asked to work in one of the company's shore-based salons prior to being offered a place on one of the ships. Employees are usually contracted for six months to two years, the latter being the maximum length of time that companies feel therapists can cope afloat. At the end of their stint on board the therapists are usually offered an opportunity elsewhere with the company.

Work on board ship can be very hard. The hours are long and you have to keep smiling, and working, when you are feeling as seasick as the passengers with whom you are sympathizing! The working conditions can be a little cramped, although often luxurious. The busiest time is just before the ship is about to dock at a scheduled port of call, as this is the time when most passengers wish to wipe away the ravages of the sea.

There are advantages to this working environment, and the obvious one is being able to see some of the world. However, since you will probably be exhausted after your long stint of work, you may find acting the tourist a little daunting, but well worth it just for two years.

There will be a great variety of treatments for you to undertake: plenty of massage and facials with a little waxing and electrolysis (less than in a high street salon). The passengers have time to indulge themselves and are often more adventurous at sea than on land.

### Yvonne comments on working on board ship

I have really enjoyed my time on board ship so far. I renewed my contract after the first six months and hope to go on doing so for the next two years or so. I usually work for five months then take one month off for a rest. I have seen a lot of the world and feel I have gained plenty of experience. I have also met a lot of nice people; I even met my fiancé through the company. He is a hairdresser and I met him on one of my trips. We were the only two working in the salon on that trip as it was a small ship, so we had to spend a lot of time together! We hope eventually to open our own hairdressing and beauty salon, but of course that will be when we have saved up enough money. In the meantime we don't see each other often as the company will not put people who are involved in a relationship on the same ship.

This is one of the major disadvantages of working on a ship: it wrecks your social life. It can be hard on your friends if you don't see them for five months at a time. Sometimes the accommodation is not too great, either – cramped and depressing – but it does depend on the ship. My last trip had me in a cabin of my own with a port-hole! The modern ships are the best. The good trips are those on which you are given full privileges, which means that you can go where the passengers go in your free time and use all the facilities that they use. On other trips you are not allowed near the passenger areas and the crew areas are not too hot. How you spend your time really does depend on the line. Of course, when you have full privileges and can mix with the passengers they don't always realize that you are off duty and there to enjoy yourself; you find yourself booking appointments for the next day and offering beauty advice in the bar.

Hours are long when you are on board, 8.30 am until 7.00 pm; fortunately we do get a two-hour lunch break. There are no days off when you're at sea either, and the days off when you're in port depend on the manager/ess and how he/she feels, but we certainly don't get all port days off.

I'd say you have got to be fairly independent and very confident. I'm not sure where I'm off to next, I'm waiting to hear. Eventually they'll let me know where I'm headed and what flight I have to take to meet my ship. I usually meet my colleagues when I arrive at the ship. The money is OK, about the same as a high street beauty salon, but of course I have no living expenses on board and the tips are fantastic. Overall a very worthwhile experience I would say. It has certainly done a lot for me.

# Hotels in Britain and Abroad

Many resort hotels and well-known London hotels in Britain have beauty salons linked to hairdressing salons. These are usually concessions run by major hairdressing and beauty companies. They vary in size and splendour, representing the image that the hotel itself is trying to create. Smaller hotels often rent space to beauty therapists working for themselves. These therapists tend to be people who have a little work experience after their college course and who then decide to set up in business on their own.

Hotels abroad also have salons that operate in the same way as the larger companies do in Britain. They advertise some of their vacancies in the beauty industry's papers and periodicals. This is in order to attract some English-speaking staff in places where most of the clientele are English-speaking. The contracts offered usually have a time limit of around two years, which allows beauty therapists to widen their experience.

In hotels based in Britain it is possible to find employment directly after completing a college course.

# 6
# Getting that First Job

We have seen where beauty therapists work. The most glamorous options are normally available to the more experienced therapists; two years' work experience in a high street salon should prepare you for the more demanding jobs. Competition for these is fierce because there are fewer opportunities. There are far more high street salons than there are 'floating salons'! But determined applicants straight from college have been known to obtain a job in a glamorous work environment. It is really up to you.

Qualified male therapists will encounter considerable difficulties in finding employment. The majority of clients are female. Because of the nature of the work, salons can claim exception from the Sex Discrimination Act which normally ensures that vacancies are open to both male and female applicants. The privacy and decency clause allows employers to stipulate gender if the work would involve close physical contact with someone of the opposite sex. Male beauty therapists will have more opportunities in places encouraging male clients.

**Where beauty therapists are found**

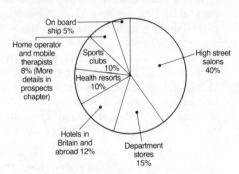

Once qualified, therapists tend to start work in high street salons to get a broad experience. Ease in finding the first job depends on where you want to work. Those in the south east find work with relative ease because of the growing number of salons.

# What to do to Find a Job

- Jobs are advertised in the beauty trade press: *The Hairdressers' Journal* (a weekly publication, available from newsagents); *Health and Beauty Salon* (a monthly magazine available on subscription from Reed Business Publishing Ltd., Oakfield House, Perrymount

Road, Haywards Heath, Sussex RH16 3DH, telephone 0444 459188).
Buy them both as soon as they come out and look at the job
advertisements. Make as many applications as you can, immediately. Remember, if offered a job that you don't like you can always
turn it down. The way to find out what a job is like is by visiting,
having a tour and meeting the staff. *Do not make your decision
merely from the advertisement.*

● You should prepare a Curriculum Vitae (a personal information
chart). It should contain the following:

personal details: name, address, contact telephone numbers, date of
birth;
educational details: schools and colleges attended, qualifications
taken and obtained;
work details: previous relevant and also irrelevant work experience,
both full- and part-time;
closing statement: why you feel that you will make a good employee and beauty therapist.

The CV should be well presented, typed if possible. Send it, with a
covering letter, to salons where you would like to work. The
covering letter should include your reasons for wanting to work in
that salon. You could get the addresses by visiting nearby towns and
establishing which salons are in the vicinity, or by going through
the Yellow Pages telephone directory.

Having written the letter don't forget to follow it up with a
telephone call to remind the employer that you require a response.
If they do not have a vacancy at the time ask them to notify you if
one arises. Make sure you speak to someone in charge, either the
owner or a member of the management team. Members of staff are
not always aware of the current situation.

● Ensure that your family and friends are on the look-out for suitable
vacancies for you. Brief them about the kinds of things that you
want and don't assume that they already understand your needs.
Your college will often receive vacancies direct from employers.
Keep in touch with them. Staff time is often limited, therefore the
responsibility to keep in touch lies with you.

● Local papers carry advertisements. If you cannot afford to buy them
all, visit your local library to scan them. Act on the day of
publication.

*Be determined, patient and enterprising. You will find something.* If
you don't, seek further advice about job-seeking skills from your
college, Careers Office or Job Centre.
*Good Luck.*

# 7

# A Typical Client

Clients vary according to the establishments they visit, although those that visit health farms regularly may also attend beauty salons in high streets on a weekly basis. The beauty therapists to whom you have been introduced in the first part of the book have each talked about their typical client. By now you should be aware of the types of client you are likely to meet if you decide to become a beauty therapist. Do the following quiz to see how much you remember.

**Typical Clients**
(Delete the inappropriate words)

- Joanne works in a *high street salon*. Most of her clients are female/male/a mixture. The treatment she offers regularly is massage/electrolysis/make-up. Most of her clients see her occasionally/regularly, which she prefers to seeing them rarely/all the time.

- Yvonne works *on board ship*. She meets a variety of people/ the same type of people on all the ships she goes on. She offers a wide variety of treatments/all body massage to the passengers who like/dislike to indulge themselves.

- Janine works for a *department store* salon where the treatments she offers are similar to/different from those offered by a high street salon. The clients are mainly local people/tourists/a mixture.

- On *health farms* the clients attend regularly/attend less than once a year. When they are visiting they see the same therapist/a different therapist for each treatment. They are all female/male/a mixture, as are the therapists and other employees.

Were you able to delete the inappropriate words without too much trouble? If you had difficulty then you should remember the following:

All treatments take at least half an hour, the more exotic treatments can take much longer. To be fully effective most require a number of visits to a therapist. Therefore those that attend regularly often have time on their hands.

The cost of having regular treatments is fairly expensive. It is therefore necessary to be well off to indulge in the more therapeutic treatments.

Most treatments are aimed at women, particularly the hair remov-ing and facial treatments.

The category of people that fit this description best are middle-class women who are not working, thus having time on their hands. Obviously this does not mean that as a beauty therapist you would meet only middle-class women. There are many other types of people who have treatments for a mixture of reasons, for example many younger women will have their legs waxed regularly.

**The age range of people attending beauty salons regularly**

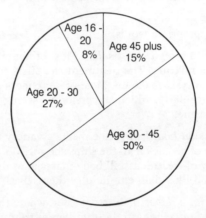

**Joanne comments on a typical high street salon client**

Most of my clients are between the ages of thirty and forty years. They tend to be middle-class women. About 50 per cent are professional working women, the rest are women who have enough cash to spend money on themselves. We sometimes have clients who have saved up for six weeks or so in order to treat themselves. They are the most satisfying to work on because if they come back to you, you know that you gave them real pleasure by giving them good service.

# 8

## What are the Prospects?

There are a number of options open to experienced beauty therapists who aspire to greater things. As we have already noted from the comments made by the beauty therapists quoted in this part of the book, staying a beauty therapist is not particularly profitable as the wages are poor. Other factors also affect the decisions made by beauty therapists to further their career. These may include a desire to be one's own boss or a need to reach one's optimum level of ability.

This chapter will deal with some of the alternatives open to beauty therapists. Those in Part Two of the book are quite separate jobs not needing beauty therapy training. The following list will give you ideas about opportunities – if they interest you do some more research; not all the areas are covered in this book.

Starting your own beauty salon   p.59

Mobile beauty therapist or home operator   p.62

Make-up artist (Part Two)   p.94

Beauty Journalist

Alternative Therapist (Part Two)   p.84

Masseur/Masseuse (Part Two)   p.92

Sales Representative   p.64

Teaching beauty at private beauty schools and further education colleges   p.65

Taking exercise classes

## Starting Your Own Beauty Salon

Starting up in business is the aspiration of many beauty therapists. However, few actually see their dream come true because, as they become more heavily involved in the industry, they become aware of the risks associated with being their own boss. Because the industry has become particularly popular over the last few years it would appear to be a good and safe investment; in fact it is, but only for those people who have spent time and money on planning and research. All businesses need a good base if they are to succeed.

There are two ways of starting your own beauty salon. The first is by becoming a franchisee with a major company. This means that you use their name and products. There is an initial capital outlay to the company, for which you receive assistance in setting up the business. The cost will vary depending upon the company that you franchise with, but the following will give you some idea of where the costs will fall.

The initial fee to the company will probably cover the design of the shop, advice on equipment needs, necessary training and assistance with the launch. In addition, the company will probably help you find a suitable site for your salon and give the necessary assistance with financial planning so that you can approach your bank manager if you require a loan. The cost of fitting out your salon, furnishing and decorating it, is down to you, as is the purchase of initial stock.

The advantages of this method are that you are selling a recognized product and you are operating under a recognized trade name. This means you do not have to begin by building up a reputation for your operation. It is therefore important to find out what sort of reputation the franchise company has and what services it is offering you. They should offer you advice while you are operating, so check out carefully the support you will receive. The disadvantage is that you are obliged to purchase products only from the franchisor, which means you are unable to shop around for the best deal. In addition, it is possible that some of your profits may have to go to the franchisor for the services they provide. It may be possible to get such services cheaper elsewhere. You will need to weigh up the pros and cons.

The alternative to this is setting up in your own right. There are three ways in which you can do this. The first, which will be discussed later, is the mobile or home operating therapist. The second is fairly common: therapists rent space from a hairdressing salon and operate from there. They are self-employed but have the advantage of an already established clientele calling in at the hairdressing salon. The third and most complex method is setting up a salon or buying an already existing one.

The practicalities of this last option must be considered very carefully before you embark on it. The type of salon services, the most appropriate location, the number of staff and so on must all be decided. It will be worth your while to seek advice, because unlike being a franchisee where the advice is built into the system, you are on your own with this method. There are organizations that offer advice to those wishing to set up a business in the beauty industry. For details of these look in the beauty press. The initial costs of seeking this advice can be offset against the long-term benefits of a successful business.

There are also organizations that will give you free advice. Some local authorities have departments to help those who wish to set up in business. They may advise you on the most appropriate way of going about this, or offer you accommodation at a cheaper rate initially. There is also an organization called the Small Firms Service which will provide you with suitable training and advice.

Obtaining finance is the next issue to consider. Often you will obtain information on this from the above-mentioned organizations. Most will tell you that you need to have some capital of your own; it is unlikely that you will receive a loan for the whole cost of your venture. The Training Commission's Action for Jobs scheme has a programme whereby they offer you a weekly income during your first year of trading. There are rules and regulations that you need to fulfil to qualify, but it is certainly worth while enquiring at your local Jobcentre for details of the scheme.

At the end of this section there is a list of addresses to enable you to start your research. Remember that you have to be really committed to any venture if it is to succeed. It will take up a lot of your spare time and will require a lot of support and understanding from your family and friends.

### Begin your plan now

What are my reasons for beginning this venture? (A hobby; to fill my spare time; an investment; to start a new career?) Are they the right reasons?

How much time am I prepared to devote to this?

Do I have any initial capital to invest in this? If not, where will I get some?

Where will I establish the salon?

Is it a good location? Are there other salons in the area? How many home and mobile operators are there in the area? Are the people in the area interested in beauty?

What sort of treatments/services do I want to offer and why?

What sort of premises will be suitable?

Do I want to go it alone or should I find out more about franchising?

What professional services will I need, for example accountants, solicitors?

How much will it all cost?

If you decide to start your own business I wish you lots of success.

### Where to find out more

For information on franchising there is an exhibition held annually in London called The National Franchise Exhibition, where franchise companies talk to interested parties about their organization and how it works. For more information on the exhibition and a list of reputable franchise companies, contact:

British Franchise Association
75A Bell Street
Henley-on-Thames
Berkshire

If you are considering setting up in business on your own, contact the Small Firms Service by phoning Freephone Enterprise.

## Mobile Beauty Therapists or Home Oper

Becoming a home operator or mobile beauty therapist are two ways of setting up in business on your own without too great an investment. Many therapists who have been working in a salon reach a point where their annual income is not going to rise any more. They have reached their optimum in terms of weekly commission on product sales, and if they are lucky enough to earn commission on the treatments that they are doing, they reach a stage where they have continuous appointments and are therefore unable to earn any more. Since the money earned in a salon is unlikely to make a therapist rich, some look for alternatives.

In addition, those who wish to increase their salary are often those who would like to work on a more flexible basis, allowing them more time to devote to other things. This is particularly true of mothers with small children.

It is obviously a big jump from the security of a nine-to-five job to working for yourself and wondering whether you are going to be able to build up a large enough client group to make yourself a reasonable income. In addition, there are the costs of the initial outlay for essential equipment. Borrowing from a bank can be worrying, and these days there are many Government schemes that will assist the entrepreneur to start a business; it is always worthwhile checking with your local Jobcentre or Careers Office for details of schemes in your area. Some schemes will pay towards your salary for the first year. Banks are ready to listen to new ideas if you present them with a good business plan; it is worth spending time on one and perhaps seeking advice before approaching your bank, so that you are really prepared to answer all the questions they will ask.

Some beauty therapists prefer to be mobile, spending all their time visiting clients at home; others set up a room in their own house which they invite clients to for treatments. Many do a combination of the two, which offers the client the opportunity to choose the method best suited to their needs, depending on the facilities available. A home operator needs the necessary equipment and enough space to allow for privacy; a couch, a trolley for waxing, a make-up tray and space to store products must all be provided. Mobile therapists need a car large enough to take all the equipment mentioned above. In addition, there will be the cost of advertising your services in local papers and newsagents' windows and of having price lists printed. These need to look professional in order to give the client the right impression.

The client group that a mobile therapist deals with consists of mothers with young children who cannot easily get to the salon; business women who cannot easily take time off during the day and like the convenience of being able to have treatment at unusual hours, and wealthy women who want to be treated in the comfort of their own homes.

The treatments that a mobile or home therapist will be able to offer will be restricted by the amount of equipment that they can buy initially and by its weight and transportability. Many suppliers make equipment that is light and portable; much of it now comes in travelling cases, but this works out slightly more expensive. The demands made on these therapists tend to be for waxing and facials, with an occasional opportunity to do wedding make-up. It is easier for a bride to be made up in the comfort of her own home than to rush from hairdresser to beauty salon on the day of her wedding.

**Laura comments on working as a mobile therapist and home operator**

I decided I wanted to work for myself because I was fed up with earning so little and had few prospects of earning much more. I was in my third job, had built up a good client group and felt that I was quite proficient in the treatments I was able to offer. Initially I was worried about my ability to build up a client group when I started on my own; in fact that is something I still worry about; last week was really quiet. I now realize it was because we were in the middle of August and most of my clients were away on holiday; however at the time I panicked and thought perhaps I was doing something wrong. This week I have been rushed off my feet. A great relief!

I like the flexibility of working for myself. I can choose my own hours, although at first I agreed to any time that the client wanted so that they would come back to me. But I'm beginning to take control now and am giving myself Monday off, working Tuesday and Wednesday during the afternoon and evening and then working all day Friday and Saturday; that way I can meet the needs of most clients. The worry of where the next client will come from has been a major disadvantage, but they always appear; and I also sometimes miss having colleagues to gossip with. But all in all I prefer it this way and I've met a lot of nice people.

I had to do a lot of research at first. I looked into insurance for myself in case I was sick and could not work, insurance in case I had an accident with a client and insurance for my equipment, which cost my savings of about £1,500. I have set up a pension plan as well. Trying to find the most appropriate equipment also involved research. My mother and I went to beauty exhibitions to look for suitable equipment and beauty products for me to use and sell to my clients. Taking my mother was helpful as this gave the older woman's perspective as well as that of a beauty therapist. We chose a range that we both liked and obviously the one that offered the best deal. At first I only bought the products I needed to use until I was sure that I would be able to sell, and of course I didn't have enough money to buy much.

Most of my clients have waxing or facials. This spring I'm doing a lot of pedicures as people are getting ready to expose their feet in summer sandals! I enjoy doing pedicures more than manicures because most people neglect their feet terribly all year round so I can see a major difference after I have done the treatment, which is very satisfying. I have done about eight wedding make-ups since I started ten months ago.

I call myself a beauty therapist in my advertising. I don't say that I'm mobile because I'd rather work in my own room at my parents' home, but I'm very careful not to put anyone off and will be flexible. I don't have women with children come to my beauty room if I can help it; I'd rather go to their homes because the children tend to run riot here. I keep up-to-date by reading beauty publications to ensure that I'm offering the most appropriate and modern treatments to my clients.

# Sales Representative

Selling is a skill the beauty therapists learn on the job. They have to sell both treatments and products to their clients. A natural extension of these skills is to become a sales representative for a company that either specializes in a particular range of cosmetics or sells beauty equipment to beauty establishments.

The attractions to some therapists are a new challenge; an interest in particular products or equipment; a chance to move about the country; and of course there is a financial incentive as representatives are usually well paid and can earn good commission. The perks are good – after an initial training period representatives receive the use of a company car.

There are no specific qualifications required to do the job, but personal qualities are extremely important. An ability to talk confidently to people and to put yourself forward, often without an invitation, are essential. A knowledge of the beauty industry is important, although there are representatives who do not have a background in the industry who are very successful.

Training usually takes place on the job. You will spend some time with an experienced member of the company prior to going on the road alone. You will probably be allotted an area of the country in which you are the sole operator. The size of the area depends very much on the size of the company: the larger the company the smaller the geographical area allotted to each representative. Product training takes place in-house and is covered in great depth so that you can speak knowledgeably to your customers.

# Electrologist

Many beauty therapists become specialists in one of the treatments in which they were originally trained. The effect of unwanted hair on some people can have a damaging psychological effect, and because electrolysis is such an important treatment for this the National Health Service employ specialists in some hospitals to undertake it. In France the treatment is only offered by members of the medical profession, and beauty therapists are not licensed to do the treatment.

The skills required to be an electrologist for the Health Service are the same as those required of beauty therapists in beauty salons, but greater emphasis is put on the personal qualities of the therapists and their manner with patients. The financial rewards are not that much better than those of a beauty therapist working in a beauty salon. However, the personal rewards and job satisfaction are considerable.

# Teaching Beauty Therapy

Qualified and experienced beauty therapists sometimes like to pass on their skills to new entrants to the profession. Some obtain jobs as trainers with large hairdressing and beauty salons. This involves inducting new beauty therapists into the company's particular method of operating. They would not train people to be beauty therapists from scratch.

Most teachers or lecturers at private schools of beauty and those lecturing in beauty at further education colleges have been beauty therapists themselves, normally for a number of years. Some of them will have obtained their posts without having been trained as teachers or lecturers, but the trend is for training establishments to employ only those who have a teaching qualification to complement their beauty therapy experience.

There are now two methods of training to teach beauty therapy. The first is to undertake a full- or part-time course leading to a Certificate in Education awarded by the Council for National Academic Awards (CNAA). The full-time course lasts for one year; the part-time course is aimed at those people already in teaching posts, and can be undertaken on a day release basis over a year-and-a-half or on an evening basis over a three-year period. These courses are run by Local Education Authority colleges of higher education. The entry qualifications are normally O-levels or GCSEs (grades A, B or C) in English and Maths; no others are normally specified although they would usually expect applicants to be qualified beauty therapists with about five years' beauty therapy experience. The Certificate in Education does not include instruction on the subject matter; its aim is to prepare people in the techniques of teaching and lecturing. The course includes an element of teaching practice attached to a further education college, in order to exercise the skills learned in class. This is the most comprehensive course of those mentioned and is recognized more widely, particularly by Local Education Authorities.

The City and Guilds of London Institute also offer a qualification (City and Guilds 730), which is studied on a part-time evening basis. The course usually lasts for one year. There is no examination at the end of the course as students undergo continuous assessments. This qualification is aimed at teachers already in work. It is most suitable for those wishing to improve their techniques in topic delivery.

Some of the private examination bodies also offer teaching certificates for qualified and experienced beauty therapists. For information on the courses available, write to the examination boards. You will find the necessary addresses at the end of the chapter entitled 'How do Beauty Therapists Train?' (p.30).

**Where to find out more**

Useful addresses for those interested in the Certificate in Education are:

Bolton Institute of Higher Education
Chadwick Street
Bolton BL2 1JW

Huddersfield Polytechnic
Holly Bank Road
Lindley
Huddersfield HD3 3BP

Garnett College
Downshire House
Roehampton Lane
London SW15 4HR

**Janine comments on her future prospects as a beauty therapy teacher**

I recently took Biology A-level at evening classes as my aim is eventually to train to teach beauty therapy at a further education college. The teacher training course I have found doesn't require specific qualifications but does ask that all applicants have at least five years' experience in industry, which is almost what I have. The course is for one year and is full-time. I think brushing up on my sciences will help me to obtain a place. In fact I found the Biology very useful in my present job; it has given me even more knowledge to help answer my clients' questions. The training aspect of the job that I'm doing at the moment will also be useful when I make my application.

# 9

# Opportunities for Job Changers

## Acceptability by the Industry

Beauty therapy is definitely a good option for those people wishing to embark on an alternative career or for those wishing to start on a career pathway later on in life. Many salons prefer to employ mature people because they feel that mature employees will relate better to the client group and sympathize with their problems.

## Funding for Further Education College Courses

Training can be a problem because of the costs involved. Often further education colleges are prepared to accept older applicants but find that Local Education Authorities will not fund them. Because there is normally only an O-level/GCSE entry requirement, awards are not mandatory for students over eighteen. Therefore more mature people find themselves responsible for paying the fees as well as keeping themselves for the two-year period. Under present regulations there is no money available from the Department of Health and Social Security for adults attending full-time courses.

If more BTEC Higher National Diplomas become available across the country (only three exist now, and current plans indicate that this will be the case for some time), it is likely that colleges will accept more adults on their courses. These carry a mandatory award from the Local Education Authority because they require higher entry qualifications, i.e. A-levels. Some colleges may accept adults on these courses without the stipulated entry qualifications, accepting relevant work experience in lieu of A-levels. Colleges make their own decisions based on factors like the number of applicants, the mix of students on the course and so on. Some Authorities do run Access courses to prepare older applicants to return to full-time study. Such courses normally last for one year and are grantable.

# Other Methods of Training

Later entrants to the beauty industry often find that the only way to train as a beauty therapist is by attending a private beauty school. The courses are shorter in length, thus allowing the mature student to embark on a new career more quickly. The students at private schools tend to be older, or at least there is usually a wider range of ages than at a further education college. Approximately 50 per cent of the places at private schools are offered to adults. Although the cost is high, the advantage lies in the speed and intensity of the training, which allow students to enter the employment field more quickly in order to begin earning.

Training schemes operated by the Training Commission may, in some areas, offer placements for adults wishing to train as beauty therapists. It is well worth investigating at your local Job Centre to see if you are eligible for this type of training.

Finally, some private schools offer part-time training courses in the evenings and at weekends. This allows working people to attend and take a few modules each year. Obviously this can be a time-consuming way of training and requires a lot of motivation. Only you can judge whether you have the time and motivation to succeed with this method.

# 10
## So Now You Know

If you have read this part of book completely you should now know a lot about being a beauty therapist. Hopefully it has helped you to decide if it is the career for you. In case it has not and you need more time to think, I suggest you do the following.

Firstly, call in at a local further education college that has a beauty therapy course or find the nearest private beauty school and book yourself a treatment. Try having a facial if you have not had any treatments before and see what it feels like. While you are having a treatment ask the student what the job is really like. You will be under no obligation to attend the course, in fact the college or school will be pleased to see you as they are always looking for models. If you are feeling flush you could have a treatment at your local beauty salon just to get the feel of the place.

Secondly, think about the skills that the beauty therapists have talked about in this part of the book. Try and list them, as shown below, and then decide if you have the necessary qualities. It may be an idea to ask someone who knows you well to help you do this.

**?**

| Skills | I am: Above Average | Average | Below Average |
|--------|---------------------|---------|---------------|
| e.g. patience | | | |

Thirdly, here are the answers to the quiz at the beginning of this part of the book. How did you do? Check your scores; no cheating. How much have you learned? Are you surprised?

**Answers to the quiz at the start of this part of the book**

*The most popular treatment offered by beauty therapists is electrolysis.*

*Most beauty therapists train in a college or private school.*

*Most beauty therapists work in high street beauty salons.*

*Most clients tend to be in their forties.*

*Most beauty therapists remain in the job, possibly going into management.*

# PART TWO

# MORE JOBS IN THE BEAUTY INDUSTRY

The People

This second part of this book looks at other jobs in the beauty industry. In fact, although they are all related in some way to the world of beauty, some jobs have stronger links than others. The beautician, for instance, is strongly involved in beauty treatments, while the alternative therapist and masseur spend much of their time relieving people of stress and therefore deal with patients rather than clients.

Again, I should like to introduce you to some people who are involved with these other aspects of the beauty industry. They will be commenting on their roles within the industry, specifically giving you information about what they do. I hope you enjoy meeting them as much as I did.

## Introducing Jane

Jane Moss works for Carolyn Miller as a colour consultant. She has been with the company since it began operating a year ago. At present the company has six consultants based in London and the home counties. The company is expanding as interest in colour analysis grows. The company has taken an American idea and given it an instinctive British feel, which Carolyn felt it needed to be acceptable to the British public. Jane has two school-age children and feels that the role of a colour consultant fits in well with being a housewife and mother.

## Introducing Alison

Alison Gibbs is twenty-three years old and works for the Essanelle salon in Milton Keynes as an aromatherapist and reflexologist. She initially trained as a beauty therapist at Aylesbury College of Further Education. She took a two-year City and Guilds course. At school she took five O-levels, of which three were sciences, then stayed on to take an A-level in Art.

Alison had experienced various beauty treatments before her O-levels and decided then that she wanted to be a beauty therapist. During her course at college aromatherapy was taught as an additional subject which students could choose if they were prepared to pay the extra fee of £50. The course lasted two days and aroused Alison's interest in the therapy.

Alison's first job was with a naturopathic clinic in Tiringham. She was employed as a masseuse, the first beauty therapist to be employed by the clinic. Previously the practice had employed masseurs and masseuses trained specifically in that skill by the Northern Institute. (See the chapter Masseurs/Masseuses for further details.) The clinic was a medical establishment which doubled as a health club. Acupuncturists, osteopaths and those offering homeopathic medicines also worked at the clinic. Alison taught pool and body exercises as well as undertaking massage. After a year she decided to look for a job that would involve her in more beauty therapy activities, to broaden her experience. By the time Alison left, more beauty therapists had been taken on by the clinic.

Alison's next job was with a health resort. She covered all treatments and was able to develop her aromatherapy skills. She decided that to do the therapy effectively she needed to undertake further training – her initial two days had only taught her the basic moves on the back and how to mix a few of the available oils. She paid for herself to attend an aromatherapy course at the Champneys Beauty School. She attended the school for one month on two evenings each week and for the whole day every Sunday. She learnt the aims and objectives of the therapy as well as new hand movements and how to mix the essential oils. Because her interest in alternative therapies had grown, Alison then followed a course in reflexology which took two weekends and two months of practice, during which time she gathered case studies. Her skills were then examined by sitting an oral and practical exam.

Alison was able to employ her skills in aromatherapy and reflexology at the resort and gained lots of experience. Because she enjoyed it so much she decided to apply for a job where she would specialize even more, and therefore applied to Essanelle to begin their launch into alternative therapies. She is beginning to build up her clientele by doing beauty treatments and then recommending the alternative therapies to clients that would benefit from them. She has also introduced the other staff, on both the hairdressing and beauty sides, to the treatments, so that they are able to discuss them with their clients. Alison feels that eventually she will stop doing general beauty treatments and concentrate entirely on the alternative therapies.

# Introducing Helen

Helen Kliton is twenty-one years old. She trained as a beauty therapist at a private school where she took and passed ITEC examinations. She found it difficult to get a job at first because there were not many salons in the area in which she lived. She was not prepared, at that stage, to move away from her family and friends.

Eventually she found a job in a local salon, but did not enjoy the work because she was not kept busy enough. Being active is very important to Helen and so she decided to look for a job that would keep her occupied all day. When she saw a post for a manicurist at the Essanelle salon in Brent Cross Shopping Centre advertised in a local newspaper, she applied and got the job. Manicure had been one of the specialist areas which Helen had enjoyed on her beauty therapy course. Essanelle have sent her on a further training course to ensure that she is up to date with the latest techniques. The salon covers both hairdressing and beauty therapy. Helen is the only nail specialist in the salon, although of course the other beauty therapists there can undertake the treatment. Although Helen started as a manicurist, she now occasionally undertakes other treatments when the other beauty therapists are busy. She derives most pleasure from doing manicures.

# Introducing Elaine

Elaine Bacon left school with a few average-grade CSE qualifications. While at school she had worked on Saturdays in a local high street hairdressing salon. She had enjoyed it even though it had been very hard work washing hair and sweeping up after the stylists. She decided that she wanted to be a hairdresser but felt that she did not want to go through the complete apprenticeship in a salon because she was already experienced in the routine duties. She applied to do a hairdressing course at a further education college. This took her two years and led to a City and Guilds qualification in hairdressing. During the course Elaine did a little make-up work, mainly personal presentation, and learnt how to do a manicure. She found that she enjoyed these most and so she decided to undertake the third year of the course, which would train her to be a beautician.

At the end of her training Elaine wrote to many beauty salons in search of a job as a beautician, but she received negative replies as most salons at that time were looking for beauty therapists.

Elaine is now twenty-one and is working as a hairdresser at a local salon close to her home. She has managed to build up a good clientele and keeps busy.

# 12

## Beauticians

**What do you know about being a Beautician?**

| STATEMENT | TRUE | FALSE |
|---|---|---|
| 1 *A beautician offers the same treatments as a beauty therapist.* | | |
| 2 *Beauticians work in beauty salons.* | | |
| 3 *More beauticians are trained every year than beauty therapists.* | | |
| 4 *Beauticians undertake the same training as beauty therapists.* | | |
| 5 *The same entry qualifications are required for both training courses.* | | |
| 6 *Beauticians spend most of their working time doing massage.* | | |

Complete the above by putting a tick in the *true* or *false* boxes against each statement. Now read this chapter; the answers will be found in it. It is a good idea not to mark your answers until the end of the chapter.

A beautician's job is similar in many ways to that of a beauty therapist as they undertake a lot of the same treatments. Many people, even employers, confuse the terms, so it is often quite difficult to establish which job is being talked about. One difference is that beauticians specialize in treatments to the face and hands and are unable to offer electrical treatments like electrolysis. A beauty therapist can offer all treatments and specializes in body treatments.

### Treatments that beauticians offer

(For details of what these treatments involve look at Part One in the chapter entitled 'The Treatments', p.19.)

| | | |
|---|---|---|
| Facials | Eyelash tinting | Depilatory creams |
| Manicure/pedicure | Eyebrow shaping | Waxing |
| Make-up | Bleaching | Saunas and sunbeds |

# How do Beauticians Train and What Qualifications and Skills are Required?

Most of the examination boards outlined in the training chapter in Part One offer beautician training. It is a less demanding version of the beauty therapy syllabus. In fact what happens is that some of the elements of the beauty therapy course are not taught, so that there are fewer examinations.

In further education colleges a beautician course sometimes follows a two-year hairdressing course. In fact it is often impossible to get a place on the second course unless you have attended the first. Some young people who do not have the necessary entry qualifications for a full-time beauty course adopt this method of training to overcome the problem. Hairdressing courses do not usually stipulate GCSEs grade C or above or O-levels as an entry requirement. There are courses that are three years in length and cover both hairdressing and full beauty therapy, but they generally require higher entry qualifications and they cover both syllabuses simultaneously.

There are no jobs in the beauty industry that require you to work as both a hairdresser and a beauty therapist. The only reason for taking such a course is if you are unsure which career you wish to pursue. However, if you wish to become a make-up artist, a knowledge of hairdressing is an advantage and the two courses together will give you a good basis from which to start. For more information on training to be a make-up artist read the chapter entitled 'Make-up Artists', p.94.

For detailed information on the syllabuses for beautician courses write to the addresses at the end of Chapter Four in Part One (see pp. 42, 43).

**Elaine comments on attending a beautician course**

After my hairdressing course I decided to stay on and do the one-year beauty training, because having tried a little beauty during the hairdressing course I realized that it was for me. I really enjoyed the course and learnt a lot; the problem came when I tried to get a job at the end of it.

I had decided that I didn't want to continue with the hairdressing beyond doing one or two of my friends' hair in the evenings to practise my skills. I started to look for a local beautician job. There are quite a few salons in the area and I was prepared to travel to the surrounding towns so I thought I wouldn't have too much difficulty. I was wrong. All the advertisements I answered wanted someone who could do electrolysis and other body treatments which I had not covered on my course. There were very few vacancies advertised for beauticians (and those that were advertised also wanted you to be able to do electrolysis). I thought about doing a course privately to increase the skills that I had but I was unable to find the necessary money. Eventually I decided I would have to go into hairdressing after all, continuing my beauty treatments in the evenings.

I think I may do some more training, but I was never very good at the academic subjects at school and was glad to get away from them. I think I may have to do Biology O-level or one of these new GCSEs at evening classes to help me pass a course. '

# Where do Beauticians Work?

Beauticians can find employment in most of the places which employ beauty therapists, but there are not many opportunities because salon owners prefer people who are able to offer every kind of treatment. For them it is more sensible financially to have all their staff trained in all the treatments.

Occasionally a salon will employ a beautician as a back-up to the beauty therapists, particularly if the client group tends to have lots of facials and manicures, in which a beautician may specialize. However, it is important to note that the trend is towards more opportunities for beauty therapists.

### Answers to the quiz at the start of this chapter

1. *A beautician offers some of the treatments that a beauty therapist offers.*

2. *Beauticians work in beauty salons as well as in other beauty establishments.*

3. *Fewer beauticians are trained each year than beauty therapists.*

4. *Beauticians undertake different training from beauty therapists.*

5. *Fewer qualifications are necessary to get on a beautician training course.*

6. *Beauticians spend most of their working time doing waxing and facials.*

# 13

# Manicurists or Nail Technicians

Those of you have experienced a manicure will know that there is more involved than simply filing and painting nails. In fact there are fashions in nails as there are in clothes; so manicurists, or nail technicians as they are sometimes known, have to ensure that they are up to date with such fashions and able to offer the latest thing to their clients.

A traditional manicure begins with the removal of nail varnish. Shaping the nails is followed by soaking them in softened water (working on one hand whilst the other is soaking) and then pushing back the cuticles and cleaning under the nail tips. Having completed the preparation, each hand is massaged for at least two minutes to the wrist or the elbow. This is a very relaxing experience. Nail varnish remover is used again to remove the hand cream used during the massage. A base coat is then applied to protect the nail from staining when the colour coat is added. The manicurist decides if the base coat needs to contain protein for weak nails. Paler colours of polish require three coats while darker ones require only two. A top coat completes the process, which normally takes half-an-hour.

Many clients will visit a manicurist once a week, others will visit before a special occasion. There are many people who take particular pride in the appearance of their nails and will make emergency appointments if they break a nail and need assistance to mend it. There are also clients who need help to prevent them from biting their nails: there are products that a manicurist can apply to make the nails taste bad. However, the aim is to make the client's nails look good so that they feel proud of them and this, many manicurists say, is enough to stop them from biting. Also, the psychological effect of having to show the manicurist bitten finger nails at the next appointment is often enough to make clients think twice before taking a nibble!

Other treatments offered by manicurists include sculptured nails, nail tips or false nails. Nail tips are the most popular at present; the manicurist attaches false nail tips from half-way up the nails, shapes them and smoothes the ridges before painting them. The process is lengthy, but the nail tips can last for up to ten weeks.

One fashion which is now dying out is that of false gold nails – often sold by jewellers as they contained real diamonds. People bought them to go on their little finger, and a woman about to be engaged would wear one on her ring finger for the night of the party.

The current trend has been inspired by American television 'soap'

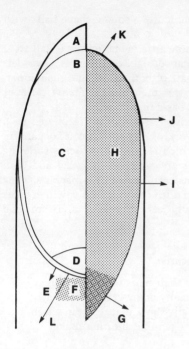

A  Free Edge
B  Dividing line/Flesh line
C  Nail plate or body
D  Lunula
E  Cuticle
F  Mantle
G  Root (matrix lies beneath)
H  Nail bed
I  Wall
J  Groove
K  Hyponychium
L  Eponychium

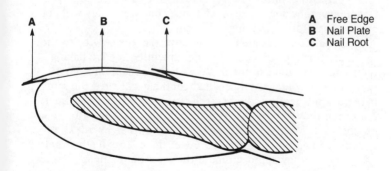

A  Free Edge
B  Nail Plate
C  Nail Root

series. This is to have a 'french manicure' – square-shape nails with the tips painted white.

The favourite treatment of the more artistic manicurist is nail art; a lengthy procedure of painting intricate designs on the nails. Considerable patience is required on the part of both client and manicurist. Obviously this is an extremely rare treatment and the main treatment undertaken by a manicurist is the basic manicure.

In the more up-market salons other treatments are offered by a manicurist which do not involve working on nails. The use of paraffin wax on the hands is something which is offered to clients suffering from arthritis. The client's hands are wrapped in gauze and then covered in very thin wax which has been heated by a machine. They are then covered by foil and a towel until the wax is cold, which takes about ten minutes. The skin usually feels very silky afterwards and the pain is often lessened.

### Helen comments on being a manicurist

These days I recognize people by their nails rather than their faces! I get hooked on clients, I really enjoy getting to know them. The older female clients really show an interest in me and in what I am doing; they are very genuine and that makes the job satisfying.

I wouldn't like to work in a hairdressing salon without the beauty side to it – I'm not sure that I would have such a regular clientele. I like to see my clients once a week or fortnight. That way we can really build up a good relationship.

I think the other advantage of working for a large company is that I earn a basic wage, whereas many manicurists do not: they take a percentage of the takings so really they are self-employed. Of course if they don't take much money one week they will not have enough for basic things like rent.

Often hairdressing salons do not advertise the service so the manicurist has to approach the clients while they are having their hair done and ask them if they want a manicure. That takes a lot of courage and personal confidence. I tried the same here but I felt really bad when they said no, which nine times out of ten they did because they hadn't planned the extra expenditure. Where I work now I have my own area with all my equipment laid out and in full view of the clients having their hair done, so they approach me if they want a manicure. Some manicurists have to keep all their equipment in a basket and move to the client.

I have very busy times: the summer and before public holidays. My clients are mainly female and middle-aged. I do have one or two male clients who have a manicure without the varnish, normally I just buff their nails with a leather buffer. I have some regular clients who are nail biters. They are often younger and have been encouraged to come here by their parents who dislike their habit. They are interesting and a challenge. If they stop biting their nails it is very satisfying for me, and nice to see their excitement and pleasure. The thing that gives me most pleasure is when I practise nail art. It takes absolutely ages – half-an-hour just for one nail. I did a lady once who was going to a Christmas fancy dress party. She had a blue sea with a red sky and a palm tree on each nail. I designed it myself.

I dislike doing pedicures: people come to me with really dirty, smelly feet and expect me to do a pedicure! I have to grit my teeth, get on with it and pretend that all is well.

I earn commission on sales of some products. We have a range of gold nails – some of them real gold. They tend to sell well at Christmas. Personally I think they look horrible, but they can earn me a lot of commission if I sell those at the top of the range.

I enjoy doing nails more than the other treatments in which I was trained, except make-up. Fortunately we have some YTS hairdressing trainees in the salon who go in for competitions, so I do their models' make-up for them. This allows me to keep my hand in.

Eventually I would like to run my own hairdressing and beauty salon, but that's a bit of a pipe dream really. I am happy here – I like the staff and the clients and have no desire to change at the moment. '

## How do Manicurists train and What Qualifications and Skills are Required?

Although there are qualifications for manicurists, it is not essential to have them in the way that it is essential for beauty therapists. Many salons, in fact, advertise for trainee manicurists.

Some manicurists have trained to be beauty therapists or hairdressers and have learnt manicure as part of the course. Having decided that either hairdressing or beauty therapy is not for them, they have used their manicure skills to get different jobs. Some hairdressers find that they have to give up hairdressing because they are allergic to the chemicals they have to use, and manicure is a useful alternative.

Hairdressing and beauty therapy courses do have examinations in manicure as part of the final examination, but the syllabus does not devote much time to manicure in comparison with the other subjects covered.

Some private schools offer manicure courses which last for one week on a full-time basis. There are also some specialist schools that train only in manicure techniques. These schools are normally linked to a specific product, but the skills covered are the same as elsewhere.

To obtain a place on a private course it is not necessary to have any specific qualifications. Employers are not particularly interested in academic qualifications either; personal skills are more important. An ability to get on with people and to converse on a variety of topics is crucial. Manual dexterity is essential because the job can be very fiddly, particularly when applying nail varnish.

**Test your manual dexterity**

Try putting nail varnish on your own finger nails. Is the left or right hand the easiest to apply? Now try applying it to someone else's nails. How much went on the nail and how much on their hands? Did you enjoy the task? Do you think you will have the patience to do this regularly?

Remember, when you are trained you will have to do the complete operation in half-an-hour. Of course you will be taught how to prevent any shaking hands that you may have experienced during our test, and with practice your application speed will increase.

# Prospects and Opportunites

There are not many opportunities for those that train solely as manicurists to progress much further. They need to train in other areas before they can move on.

Some specialist nail salons are opening up, and as this becomes more common it may increase the chances for those with the right skills to move into management. It is possible to work from home, advertising in the local papers that you are offering a manicure service. However it is likely that you will be in competition with mobile and home operating beauty therapists, who will be able to offer a wider range of treatments than you can as a manicurist. It is more convenient for most clients to see the same person for all their treatments rather than use several different specialists.

There are opportunities for mature people; employers are not particularly worried about age. The only problem that adults may encounter is the wage level which, unlike many industries, does not take age or experience into account.

# Where do Manicurists Work?

## Hairdressing salons

The majority of manicurists work in hairdressing salons. There is a tendency for smaller salons to invite a manicurist to work on a self-employed basis. The salon negotiates with the manicurist the hours of work required, an appropriate price to charge and what financial benefits the salon will receive from having the manicurist on the premises. The salon then advertises the additional services available to their clients; the rest is up to the manicurist. At first it can be hard for people working in these conditions because there may be no income until they have built up a regular client group.

Furthermore, as someone who is self employed the manicurist must calculate the tax and National Insurance contributions required. Therefore it is important to think carefully before embarking on such a venture. It is worth taking advice from an appropriate agency (see Chapter 8, p.62) if you decide this is the way you wish to work. This method does, of course, give the manicurist a lot of freedom and often a greater incentive to work harder because more of what he or she earns goes into his or her pocket and not that of an employer.

Larger salons employ manicurists on a normal wage system. The wages are never very good but salons offer commission on sales as an incentive. When combined with tips, this can raise the income considerably.

## Beauty salons

Beauty salons tend not to employ manicurists as the beauty therapists undertake this along with their other treatments. A salon will occasionally take on a receptionist who is trained in manicure so that they can offer it as an extra service without taking the therapist away from more profitable treatments. Beauty salons linked with hairdressing salons are more likely to employ specialist manicurists.

## Specialist nail salons

In some of the major cities it is possible to find salons that offer only manicure and pedicure, selling the products to go with it. These are more likely to offer to train new staff to do the treatments, while beauty salons will probably be looking for staff who are already trained. The specialist salons employ staff as well as having people who work on a self-employed basis. In reality few such places exist at present; it is only more recently that manicure as a treatment in its own right has become popular. It still isn't well enough established to offer many opportunities for people entering it as a career.

# 14
## Alternative Therapists

### Reflexologists

Reflexology is said to be an ancient Eastern therapy, and is based on the idea that each area of the foot corresponds to a particular area of the body. Therefore if you have tension in your neck, there is an area of the foot (just at the base of your big toe) which, if massaged, will ease your neck. Having recently experienced a half-hour of foot massage, I was surprised to find how relaxed I felt after it!

Reflexology works in a similar way to acupuncture, in that it is based on the energy channels in the body. There are reflex points in the foot which link through the energy channels with reflex points in other parts of the body. If mental or physical stress cause these channels to become blocked, the energy cannot pass freely through the body. This can cause illnesses, which are manifestations of these blockages. The aim of reflexology is to keep the channels clear so that the natural energy in the body can flow freely, thereby preventing illness.

A reflexology treatment can also be done on the head and hands, but the most sensitive areas are the feet and therefore they are used most frequently. Normally a reflexologist will only treat the hands or head if the client has a foot problem, for example a bad case of athlete's foot.

Each area of the foot is carefully massaged, concentrating on the pressure points. A reflexologist can tell if you are having particular problems with a certain part of your body by the way parts of your feet feel to them under pressure, and the way the skin reacts. If there is a lot of tension in a specific part of the foot, it is likely that the client will be experiencing problems with the corresponding part of their body. As with all alternative therapies, the practitioner has to be careful not to alarm the client when discussing the areas for concern. Reflexologists are not medical practitioners and therefore do not usually diagnose particular ailments. The emphasis is always on professional behaviour.

In many instances reflexology is combined with aromatherapy, because the reflexology part of the treatment can diagnose problem areas to be worked on with aromatherapy. Because of this it is possible to find reflexologists in beauty salons, the reflexologist and aromatherapist being one and the same person.

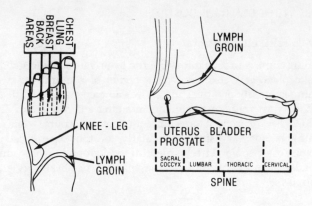

CHEST
LUNG
BREAST
BACK
AREAS

KNEE - LEG

LYMPH GROIN

LYMPH GROIN

UTERUS PROSTATE   BLADDER

SACRAL COCCYX | LUMBAR | THORACIC | CERVICAL

SPINE

# INTERNATIONAL INSTITUTE of REFLEXOLOGY

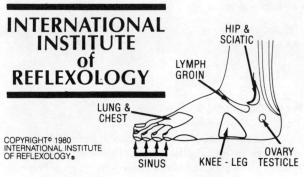

HIP & SCIATIC

LYMPH GROIN

LUNG & CHEST

SINUS

KNEE - LEG

OVARY TESTICLE

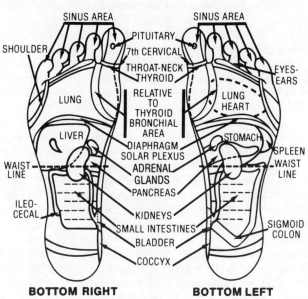

SINUS AREA

SINUS AREA

SHOULDER

PITUITARY

7th CERVICAL

THROAT-NECK THYROID

EYES-EARS

LUNG

RELATIVE TO THYROID BRONCHIAL AREA

LUNG HEART

LIVER

DIAPHRAGM SOLAR PLEXUS

STOMACH

SPLEEN

WAIST LINE

ADRENAL GLANDS

WAIST LINE

PANCREAS

ILEO-CECAL

KIDNEYS

SMALL INTESTINES

BLADDER

COCCYX

SIGMOID COLON

**BOTTOM RIGHT**

**BOTTOM LEFT**

85

## How do reflexologists train?

Training courses in reflexology are run by private schools and normally take place at weekends over a period of a month or two. The training is mainly practical and carries no recognized qualification at the end. Most training establishments offer a certificate or diploma, awarded by the school on completion of the course. The cost of training is not excessive, particularly for the experienced beauty therapist or people with a medical background, who would not normally have to cover any of the anatomy or physiology elements required.

## Where to find out more

The Institute of Reflexology
PO Box 34
Harlow
Essex CM17 0LT

# Aromatherapists

Aromatherapy has its origins in ancient Egypt, where the medical uses of essential oils were well known. It became popular recently after the publication of a book written by a French chemist called René Gattefosse who experimented with essential oils earlier this century.

The basis of the therapy is a combination of a special massage technique and the use of essential oils. The oils penetrate the skin through the capillaries and lymphatic network, reaching the adjacent organs. Aromatherapists say the nose and the skin conduct the oils, with their rejuvenating benefits, to the areas where they are most required.

The essential oils are plant extracts; each plant has a specific healing property. The production of these essential oils is expensive because each flower can only supply a single drop. The oils are extracted by a steam distillation process; steam is passed through the plant at low pressure and as it cools the oil separates out. The really precious flowers are treated differently; the technique for extracting the oil is more complicated and thus the product is much more expensive. Before use, the essential oils are diluted with a pure vegetable oil. The carrier/base oil prevents burning or irritation to the skin. The aromatherapist decides what proportion of each oil should be used, according to the needs of the particular client. The vegetable oil base can take many forms, each having its own benefit – for example almond oil or peach kernel oil for the delicate areas like the face.

The essential oils are divided into three types. The first type is the strongest and therefore has instant impact; the second has a longer-lasting aroma with a dominant effect; the third has a lingering subtle effect. A combination of three oils, one from each category, will have the greatest benefit. The following chart gives you examples of the types of oils used, and shows which can be blended together to give the greatest benefit for particular ailments:

| AILMENT | OIL ONE | OIL TWO | OIL THREE |
|---------|---------|---------|-----------|
| Acne | Lemongrass | Lavender | Sandalwood |
| Headaches | | Rosemary or Lavender (choice will depend on type of headache) | Sandalwood |
| Arthritis and rheumatic aches and pains | Sage | Rosemary | Sandalwood |
| Nervous disorders: tension stress | Bergamot | Lavender | Sandalwood, or Ylang Ylang if frustration is present. |

Many ailments are stress-related, so the use of calming oils like lavender is fairly common. The chart only shows a few of the ailments that can be treated by aromatherapists and only a very few of the oils they can use.

Aromatherapists have traditionally blended their own oils, but more recently companies have been set up to sell therapists oils that have already been blended for particular ailments. They have also created ranges of essential oils as bath oils, aromatic body oils and vaporizing oils. The intention is to encourage the aromatherapists to sell the oils to their clients for use between treatments.

The treatment begins with a verbal examination to establish which part of the body the client believes is causing problems. This is followed by a physical examination of the client's back to diagnose the condition of the skin. The aromatherapist runs his or her fingertips up and down the spine to see if any redness occurs. Each vertebra corresponds to a part of the body, therefore if redness occurs in a particular area the therapist knows which part of the body requires treatment. Having located the problem areas, the therapist knows which oils to blend. The massage begins, using a combination of pressure movements with the knuckles and fingertips and circular movements towards the glands to assist drainage, and working on either side of the spine to relax the nerve endings. The ultimate aim is to help clear energy pathways in the body.

Aromatherapists frequently also study other alternative therapies, thereby giving them the flexibility to develop treatments tailor-made to the individual. The length of a treatment, therefore, will vary. The average time is from one hour to one-and-a-half hours. The frequency of the treatments will depend very much on the individual client's needs.

Often the benefits are not immediately apparent, although the advantages of having a massage will be felt straight away. The real effect can take anything up to two days to be realized.

### Where do aromatherapists work?

Aromatherapists can be found in a number of working environments. In fact the majority work in the same establishments as beauty therapists. For more details turn to Part One of the book and read Chapter 5, p.45. Aromatherapists also work from home and in specialist aromatherapy clinics. The latter often also offer other alternative therapy treatments.

### How do aromatherapists train?

There are no courses running at further education colleges which are specifically aimed at people wishing to be aromatherapists. Most training takes place in private establishments, often private beauty schools. The courses vary in length and in price. They do not, however, differ very much in the entry requirements they make. In most cases applicants must either be trained beauty therapists or have a medical background such as nursing, in order to cope with the physiology involved. There are no recognized qualifications, but there are organizations to represent the industry, to which suitably trained aromatherapists can belong. Membership of the International Federation of Aromatherapists is dependent on a minimum number of hours' training and experience in massage. The Federation will supply you with a list of schools offering training in aromatherapy; their address is near the end of this section, p.89.

Some further education colleges are offering training in alternative therapies as part of a full beauty therapy course. An additional charge is often made for a one- or two-week course. Most courses at private schools are short and can be followed on a part-time basis.

**Where to find out more**

International Federation of Aromatherapists
46 Dalkeith Road
West Dulwich
London SE21 8LS

The Association of Aromatherapists
44 Ditchling Rise
Brighton BN1 4QN

**Alison comments on being an aromatherapist and reflexologist**

Initially I wanted to be a beauty therapist, until I did a two-day course on aromatherapy at college which I found very interesting. As I learnt more I felt that I was able to offer a better service to my clients if I gave them aromatherapy treatment rather than a traditional beauty treatment. I really enjoy practising aromatherapy; I always liked body work more than facials, and I find this much more rewarding as it really does help my clients. I find that they are prepared to undergo aromatherapy if they have a problem because they consider it a medical treatment, while beauty therapy is often seen as an indulgence.

I prefer to combine my reflexology treatments with aromatherapy. I begin with reflexology in order to locate any problem areas a client might have. This could be stress, which would show when I touched certain pressure points on the feet. A reflexology treatment lasts half-an-hour. I then suggest the client returns the next week to undergo an aromatherapy treatment, during which I work on the areas already identified as problems. This is not to say that these cannot be found without reflexology, because they can; however the two together have a very beneficial effect.

I once had a client who burst into tears half-way through an aromatherapy treatment. She was an older woman who had lost her husband six months previously and who, having kept all her emotion bottled up inside her, had become very tense. Releasing the tension unleashed her emotions. This had a very healthy effect on her and she continued to come for treatment.

People say you have to be strong to do a treatment but I don't think so. I find that, because the movements are slow and rhythmical, and are pressure movements, it's not necessary to be strong. After all, I'm only slight in build and don't have lots of bulging muscles! Most of the time you're working through the energy channels in the body; once these have been stimulated they do the rest of the work. The benefits are felt after two or three days, not immediately.

My clients are similar to those who regularly attend for beauty treatments; that's because I work in a beauty salon. They are mainly middle-aged women who may be suffering from menopausal problems; I can help balance out their hormones. A positive attitude to the treatment is essential; sceptics rarely benefit. With both treatments people experience different effects at the time; some feel rejuvenated, others feel low for a few days. But most benefit in the long term.

# Other Alternative Therapies

There are many other alternative therapies; some are better known than others. the two that I have outlined above are the most widely used at present in the world of beauty. Because many of the others may be associated more with medical practitioners than with beauty, I shall only mention them briefly and then give you sources to follow up yourself.

## Acupuncture

Acupuncture is the best-known alternative therapy, and many other therapies have evolved from it. It involves the use of fine needles to stimulate 'acupuncture points' and encourage energy to flow through the 100 or so channels in the body. For more information contact:

British Acupuncture Association and Register
34 Alderney Street
London SW1V 4EU

## Spinal touch

This is based on a belief that a misalignment in the back creates all kinds of ailments. Put simply, the aim of spinal touch is to relax the muscles which have caused this misalignment, allowing the spine to return to its normal position and so relieving any ailments. The therapist works on 'touch zones', which are similar to those areas used in acupuncture and aromatherapy, to release the muscle tension.

## The Alexander Technique

This is said to be a complete physical re-education of the body. The continual misuse of our bodies in everyday life eventually results in aches and pains. The Alexander technique is a retraining for our bodies so that we learn to use them correctly. Little manipulation is used. Once educated, clients experience both physical and emotional well-being. Further information is obtainable from:

The Society of Teachers of the Alexander Technique
3B Albert Court
Prince Consort Road
London SW7

## Auricular therapy

This is very similar to reflexology, in that auricular therapists believe that each area of the body has a corresponding reflex in the ear. These points are stimulated by a laser or electrical current of a highly sophisticated form. Further information is obtainable in books sold by:

The Asia Acumedic Company
103 Camden High Street
London NW1

The following list is of those therapies that are definitely not part of the beauty world; their title and a contact address is available for further research.

## Homeopathy

The British Homeopathic Association
Basildon Court
27A Devonshire Street
London W1N 1RJ

## Naturotherapy and Osteopathy

British Naturotherapy and Osteopathic Association
6 Netherhall Gardens
London NW3 5RR

# 15

# Masseurs/Masseuses

This is a career that is becoming increasingly popular as the demand for masseurs and masseuses grows. Massage has become a well-known and accepted method of relaxation, and can cure many muscular aches and pains.

Massage also forms a part of many of the alternative therapies listed in the preceding chapter, as well as being an important element in the work of a beauty therapist. For details of what massage involves read Chapter 3, p.21.

Training in the art of massage is essential; it is not something which anyone can undertake because they have rubbed soneone's back in the past and the recipient enjoyed it. It is important to have a complete understanding of both anatomy and physiology, as an incorrect massage can have an adverse effect on the organs of the body and on the skeleton. A massage that has been done properly can be beneficial to both these areas as well as many others.

Swedish massage is the technique taught in many beauty schools, based on the research carried out by a Swedish professor. The term 'remedial massage' is often used to distinguish massage that has a therapeutic effect, solving ailments, from a body massage, one carried out after a steam bath or sauna to stimulate the skin.

## How do Masseurs/Masseuses Train

Many masseurs and masseuses train as beauty therapists and then specialize later on in their career. Others take specialist courses run by private beauty schools. It is difficult to give guidelines about appropriate courses as there are no trade organizations or recognized qualifications. The Northern Institute is a private school which, for a number of years, has offered correspondence courses linked with practical sessions. Many of its students have found jobs as masseurs and masseuses. Other schools advertise in the beauty trade press. When considering any school it is important to ensure that the following subjects are offered: anatomy and physiology, including a complete run down of the muscular system; the vascular system; the digestive system and the complete bodily functions. A masseur/euse must be familiar with and able to deal with sports injuries like sprains, the draining of the lymphatic system necessary to reduce the effects of stress and, of course, the essential hand and body movements.

Underwater massage. ▶

The above is a very simplistic description of the training required. Any training you receive will only prepare you to work in the establishments mentioned above; none will allow you to work in the Health Service, where physiotherapists are employed to do massage along with their other tasks. A book on the medical profession will give you details of how to train for this. Physiotherapists are also employed by football clubs and other professional sports clubs in order to look after the players' injuries and give them massages.

The private schools do not suggest any minimum qualifications as entry requirements for massage courses. Only you can decide whether you feel able to cope with the academic parts of the course. Obviously, if you have taken Biology at school or college and have sat an examination in it you will be at an advantage.

Manipulative skills are very important. Many beauty therapists find massage physically tiring, and it is worth bearing in mind your personal fitness and strength when considering this as a career. To do ten massages a day in a health resort will take a lot of stamina; remember that you will be on your feet most of the time.

## here do Masseurs/Masseuses Work?

Masseurs and masseuses work in similar environments to those discussed in the beauty therapy section. These are health farms or resorts, beauty salons, sports centres or clubs, and on board ship. In addition, they work in private practice. For those prepared to travel or live in, there are numerous opportunities in cities or in health resorts in this country. Although there is a demand for masseurs and masseuses, the opportunities may not occur in your local area unless you are prepared to set yourself up in business. If you are, the advice in Chapter 8 (p.59) will apply to you.

For information about the Northern Institute courses, write to:
The Northern Institute
100 Waterloo Road
Blackpool FY4 1AW

# 16
# Make-up Artists

## What do you know?

The following statements are either true or false. Read them carefully, then make your decision by ticking the appropriate box. You should then read the chapter before looking at the answers at the end.

| STATEMENT | TRUE | FALSE |
|---|---|---|
| 1 A make-up artist works in a beauty salon or department store making up customers. | | |
| 2 A make-up artist works a nine-to-five day and does not travel away from home. | | |
| 3 All make-up artists work for one particular company. | | |
| 4 Make-up artists have to have hairdressing skills. | | |
| 5 There are lots of colleges where you can train to be a make-up artist. | | |

# The Job

Make-up artists work in a number of environments; it is the differences between these areas which dictate the type of work they do.

## Television

The area with which most of us are familiar with is television work. A television make-up artist will either be employed by the television company, particularly the larger ones, or will work on a freelance basis. The latter is more common with the smaller companies which do not actually make many of their own programmes.

A make-up artist employed by a television company undertakes a wide variety of tasks. Normally they work on a shift system, which involves them moving between different programmes, and the work required of them depends on the programme with which they are associated at any particular time. It is important to remember that any person appearing on television for whatever reason will have encountered a make-up artist before their appearance. A make-up artist will therefore have to do routine jobs like current affairs programmes or the nightly news. On such occasions their role is to ensure that the interviewer, newsreader or guest does not shine under the studio lights and that facial blemishes are not visible. An understanding of shading and highlighting techniques is taught at the start of any training course and is used in this type of routine make-up work.

A greater range of skills are required to work on a series like *EastEnders*. Here the cast are made up to be specific characters. The actor/tress will develop a character, but the make-up artist helps to give that character a visual identity. If the viewer is unaware that make-up has been applied, the artist has done a good job.

Drama series also require special effects make-up. For instance, if a character suffers some kind of injury the make-up artist helps the realism by applying a false bruise or cut to the actor/tress. Wax is used to build up the fake scar tissue and shading is added for the bruised area. The artist records the exact colours used and the precise position of the scar, to ensure continuity for the following day's shoot. Other programmes, particularly thrillers, also require this kind of work. In addition, they may also have characters who age during the course of the programme or throughout the series. The make-up artist has to learn how to effect this ageing process. Making someone of twenty look sixty is a long and laborious process – not least for the actor/tress.

The third area, for which a make-up artist will need different skills, is in the production of historical programmes. Here, it is essential that historically accurate make-up and hairstyles are used. The person in charge of the make-up team on a period piece has to do plenty of research into hairstyles and make-up long before filming actually begins. They liaise closely with the costume department to ensure continuity, and they order the manufacture of any necessary wigs.

There are many other techniques which a make-up artist may need to use; some, for example, have had to paint false tattoos on members of the cast. Those techniques already mentioned, however, are those that occur most often.

A make-up artist in television (and elsewhere) will also be expected to dress hair. This may include giving an actor a hair piece or facial hair piece. In some cases the artist will actually fabricate a piece of facial hair – a moustache, say – using wig-making techniques, although some companies employ specialists to do this work. One, based in London, made gorilla outfits – this takes months of patient work. Artists are seldom asked to cut hair and are not, therefore, expected to be fully qualified hairdressers. They will, however, need to master the basic skills so that they can style and dress hair. They will also have to know how to do some old-fashioned styles for historical work.

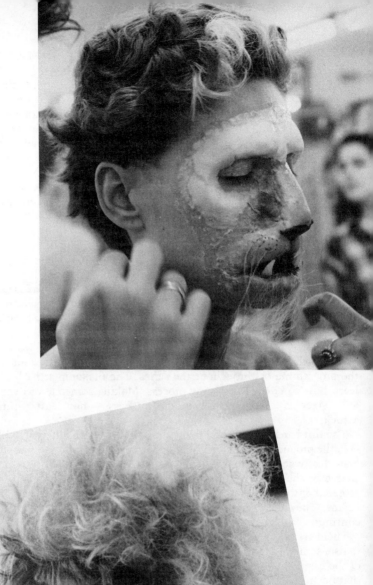

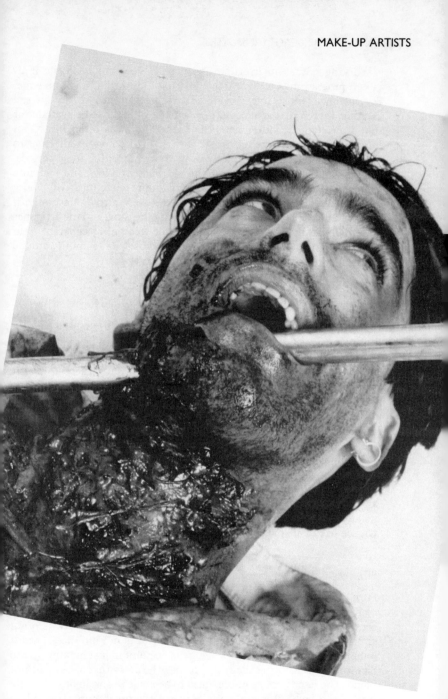

Television drama requires special make-up effects. These are by students at Complections, International London School of Make-up.

97

Working hours are irregular and depend very much on the individual programmes with which the artist is linked at any one time. For instance, most live current affairs programmes go out in the evening, therefore it is necessary for a make-up artist to be available at that time. On the other hand, historical drama is often filmed on location and the make-up artist, as part of the crew, will have to travel, often staying in hotels away from home for long periods. Shooting takes place when the light and weather allow, and therefore there are a lot of early starts – especially for the make-up artist, whose work is often done before the rest of the crew arrive. Naturally, if there is a heavy make-up to apply this can take time, and the artist has to remain on the set in case the lights or weather or constant wear affect the finished look. The rest of the day is spent standing around doing a few 'touch ups' as and when necessary.

## Theatre

Make-up skills for theatre are somewhat different. In the past a cast's make-up was extremely heavy, because it needed to be seen in poor light by members of the audience sitting quite some distance from the stage. Many actors and actresses who work in the theatre now also appear on television, and they are used to wearing much lighter bases and creams. Techniques and products have improved, and a greater realism in styles of acting, design and lighting has led to a change in the look of theatrical make-up.

Theatres tend to employ artists on a freelance basis, so that they are available when the theatre is mounting a production which requires their services. Some companies will take a make-up artist on tour with them in order to maintain the continuity. Late nights are anti-social, but this is when theatres require the services of their make-up artist, and this needs to be taken into account when anyone wishes to pursue a career in this area.

## Film

Film make-up also tends to employ artists on a freelance basis. Film companies in Britain are not in production all the time and therefore they do not keep a full crew of make-up artists. The work is often similar to that in television; in both cases it is not only facial work but often complete body work. There is no point in just making up the face and then ignoring the rest, because the areas that show will not blend. The hands, for example, need to be made up, as do other visible bits of the body. Remembering some of the programmes and films around today, it may be worth keeping this fact in mind!

### Photographic and fashion

Photographic and fashion make-up are less demanding areas for the make-up artist to enter because the skills required are fewer. Every photograph that appears in advertising, both on television and in magazines, uses models who have been made-up by a make-up artist. Here again, hairdressing skills are necessary. Sometimes the model knows what style best suits their hair and will achieve this effect without assistance, but the photographer or director may have a different image in mind and the make-up artist will be expected to create it.

Session make-up artists need to keep themselves up to date with the latest fashions. They may be required to work on a fashion show one day and a television advertisement the next. The need for flexibility and mobility is essential. It is possible to find yourself on location in Portugal working for a magazine one week, and in London the next working on a model who will appear in a photograph on a bill-board.

# Where do Make-up Artists Work?

We have talked about the environment dictating the job, and this will have given you a good idea of where make-up artists work. Large television companies tend to be the only organizations which employ full-time artists. In most other environments the make-up artist works on a freelance basis. In most cases they are either registered with an agency, which contacts them when suitable work is available, or they are well enough known in the industry not to need an agent. Those who are lucky enough to be in the latter category are contacted direct by photographers, directors or television companies for whom thay have worked before.

There are few agents who deal solely with make-up artists. Many are model agencies that have four or five artists on their books, others are film personnel agents that supply the technical crew for film sets. They, too, would only register a few make-up artists. Some artists are registered with more than one agent, so that they are kept busy throughout the year.

One of the major problems in this kind of work is establishing yourself as a make-up artist and finding an agent to represent you. This involves a lot of trailing round agents with a portfolio of your work, and requires masses of personal confidence.

# Getting that First Job

Many people aspire to be make-up artists; too many for the number of jobs available. Television companies receive thousands of letters each year from people wishing to train, and they have time to interview only a fraction of those with the right qualities and qualifications.

## Qualities

Personal qualities are very important. A make-up artist often works with actors and actresses who are waiting to play a big scene. It is important that the make-up artist be understanding and sympathetic if the recipient of their art does not wish to chat. On the other hand, if they are working for television they may have to reassure a guest speaker new to television. An ability to discern a person's state of mind is therefore of paramount importance, and is perhaps a talent which cannot be taught at a training college.

Stamina is the second quality that a good make-up artist should possess. There can be sudden bursts of frantic work, followed by long lulls during which you must stay alert in case you are needed. Standing around with little to do can be very tiring. If you are on location you may find that you have to stand in the rain and the wind, which makes the glamorous life seem very far away. Some make-up artists tell stories of making actors up in force ten gales on beaches in the middle of nowhere! Filming schedules have to be met, and the crew can find themselves shovelling away snow so that filming can continue as if it were the middle of summer. Where is the make-up artist while this is going on? Standing in the cold removing the icicles from the faces of the cast and then replenishing the make-up, assisting with the illusion that it is the height of summer!

## A portfolio

Putting together a portfolio is essential if you want to succeed. It is no good just saying what course you completed, as this will not be valued without a good portfolio. It is not even necessary to do a course if you have the skills to get a portfolio together in another way. Agents and employers will wish to see a selection of your work even if they offer some training themselves.

A portfolio should contain photographs of work that you have done over a period of years. Ideally it should include work that you did while involved with a drama group at school. It should include examples of the numerous kinds of work you may be expected to do.

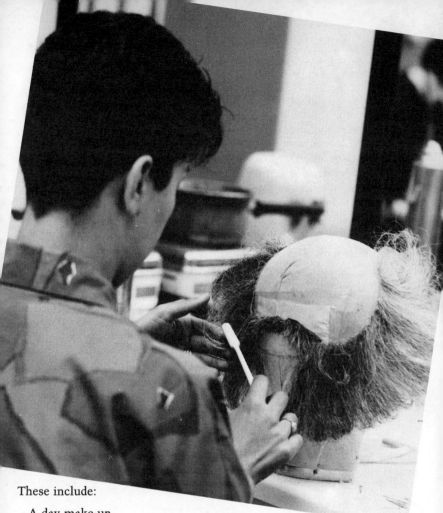

These include:

A day make-up

An evening make-up

A fashion make-up

An ageing make-up on both a male and a female (before and after shots are always useful)

Dramatic accident make-up (scarring, bruising, knife wounds, etc.)

An historical make-up

A body make-up

The photographs should be done professionally, if possible. Examples of other techniques like wig-making and false noses are also an advantage. The emphasis in the portfolio should reflect the kind of job that you are after or the type of work in which you hope to specialize.

# How do Make-up Artists Train?

This is always a difficult area, because many make-up artists are self-taught. They have learnt their skills and had the necessary confidence to sell them to agencies or directors. Few employers of make-up artists ask to see paper qualifications; they are much more interested in what relevant work you have done before. The difficulty is in getting this work experience.

There are three alternatives to the self-taught method: training with a television company, at a further education college or at a private school.

## Training with television companies

Few television companies actually train make-up artists on a regular basis. They tend to run their training schools only when they perceive a need to recruit additional staff to the make-up department.

The BBC run the biggest and most regular training school. They tend to recruit approximately twelve trainee make-up artists at any one time. This may be as often as once a year when things are going well, but in leaner times they may only recruit once every two or three years.

*Entry requirements for the BBC*

|  |  |
|---|---|
| *Age* | 20 years and 6 months |
| *Educational requirements* | A-levels, including art |
|  | *or* |
|  | Art foundation course |
|  | *or* |
|  | Fine arts degree |
|  | *or* |
|  | Hairdressing and beauty therapy qualification |
| *Plus Other Specifications* | A portfolio of work undertaken in an amateur or professional capacity. |
|  | Experience of hairdressing, particularly traditional methods like finger waves and pin curls. |
|  | Maturity and a proven ability to deal with people from all walks of life. |

The majority of people who are accepted by the BBC have a good combination of the qualifications mentioned above, as these demonstrate a good all-round ability. Few have just a hairdressing and beauty therapy qualification. Many applicants are older then the minimum age mentioned.

*The BBCs selection procedure*

Approximately 650 people apply.

▼

Application forms are scrutinized.

▼

50-60 applicants are invited for an informal chat with someone from the make-up department.

▼

All these undertake a practical test lasting about twenty minutes (it involves applicants making-up the faces and doing hair of two models).

▼

35-40 are then invited to a board interview, which normally has three panel members.

▼

12 applicants are offered places on the next make-up training course.

*The training*

The courses last three months and are based in the training school at the Elstree studio. They are very intense and cover all aspects of the work that the artist will have to do. Those who successfully complete the course become Assistant Make-up Artists attached to a team. Progression thereafter depends on personal ability. The highest grade is the Make-up Designer, who liaises with the programme director and decides on the most appropriate style for the make-up.

**Training at further education colleges**

There is in fact only one course currently offered by a further education college which trains people specifically in the work of a make-up artist. This course is available at the London College of Fashion. Because of the level of entry students on the course are able to apply for local authority grants, and applicants therefore come from all over Great Britain. The college has access to a hall of residence to which students can apply for accommodation.

The Business and Technician Education Council (BTEC) are the awarding body for the Higher National Diploma in Theatrical Studies (Theatrical Make-up Studies Option). This is a two-year, full-time course which covers make-up and hairdressing for television, theatre, film, photographic and fashion work.

*Course entry requirements*

| | |
|---|---|
| *Age* | 18 years by 1st of September of year of entry |
| *Educational requirements* | BTEC Diploma in General Art and Design<br>*or*<br>BTEC Diploma in General Vocational Design<br>*or*<br>2 GCE A-levels, including Art<br>*plus*<br>GCSEs (grade C or above) or O-levels in English and a science subject |
| *Plus Other Specifications* | A portfolio of work, to include a selection of art work and photographic work. Strong motivation to succeed as a make-up artist. |

The course includes an element of work experience, which normally means an attachment to an area of work which the student wishes to enter eventually. At the end of the course, having prepared excellent portfolios, students enter various jobs in the industry.

Competition for places on the course is very fierce, and often successful applicants have relevant work experience in addition to the minimum entry qualifications.

### Training at private schools

There are many private schools which advertise training for make-up artists. The courses are expensive and are relatively short, some only as long as six weeks. They claim to cover all the skills necessary to become a make-up artist. Because there are no recognized qualifications for this side of the beauty industry, it is extremely difficult to judge whether a particular school gives value for money or not. Whatever the quality of the training, it is very important to remember that you are the one who will have to sell your skills in a very competitive market. You will need to be very self-assured to do this; in fact you will probably have to be really pushy to get noticed. No one can train you to be in the right place at the right time.

*Things to remember when applying to private schools*
Firstly decide what aspect of the make-up business you wish to specialize in. Is it editorial – the making up of models for fashion photographers; advertising – the making up of actors/actresses/models for television and magazine commercials; or television, film and theatre – the making up of actors/actresses using ageing and numerous other techniques to achieve a dramatic effect. To have the greatest opportunities open to you it is best to develop all these skills.

Having decided, check that the school you have in mind offers all the facets of the area you wish to enter. Remember that whatever your particular field, you will need to have some hairdressing training.

Visit some schools and look at the facilities on offer. Find out what the course cost includes. Does it include use of school equipment and products, or will you have to supply your own? Do the course tutors have any background in the industry, and if so, what areas does their experience cover? Are students examined in any way at the end of the course, or does everyone who pays the fee get a certificate?

**Where to find out more**

The Business and Technician Education Council Information Service
Central House
Upper Woburn Place
London WC1H 0HH

Department of Hairdressing and Beauty Therapy
The London College of Fashion
The London Institute
John Princes Street
London W1

BBC Corporate Recruitment Services
Broadcasting House
London W1A 1AA

**Answers to the quiz at the start of this chapter**

How did you do in the quiz at the beginning of this chapter? See the answers you gave and check them against the correct answers given here:

1. *A make-up artist does not work in a beauty salon or department store making up customers.*

2. *A make-up artist does not work a nine-to-five day and does travel away from home.*

3. *All make-up artists do not work for one particular company.*

4. *Make-up artists have to have hairdressing skills.*

5. *There are not many colleges where you can train to be a make-up artist.*

# 17
# Colour and Image Consultants

Colour consultancy is a growing industry in Britain today. It is a recent import from the United States of America and is growing in popularity.

## The Job

A colour analyst is someone who examines the tones of a client's skin and categorizes him or her according to the 'International Colour Wheel'. The basic principle is that each of us has either a yellow or a blue skin base; those with a blue base fall into the 'winter' or 'summer' categories, those with a yellow base are either 'spring' or 'autumn'. Having analysed the skin, the consultant then advises the client as to the most appropriate colours to wear to enhance his or her looks. If you generally wear a mixture of colours from each of the categories, it is possible that on the days you wear the wrong colours your friends will ask you if you are ill or whether you are feeling tired. If this happens to you, you may need advice!

A true colour consultant will spend at least three or four hours with a group of clients. The idea is to work together to analyse scarves of colours from each range one at a time. It is easier for others to see which colours suit you than it is for you to see yourself. Once the analysis is completed you receive a wallet containing your range of colours, so that you have something to take with you when you are shopping for clothes. Eventually you are able to build up a wardrobe of your colours; having a colour co-ordinated wardrobe with colours that suit you apparently saves you money, because you don't need to buy different shoes and belts to go with each outfit, and every blouse or shirt should go with a selection of skirts and trousers.

Having decided on your clothes, the next thing is to decide on your image: are you a classic or a casual? It is rare to be both. There are a number of different images, but they should not be mixed. Once decided upon, the image should be maintained both at home and at work.

Private individuals often have a colour consultation session just out of pure interest. Other have it in order to enjoy greater personal success in business. The argument for this is that the first few seconds after you meet someone new is the time when they form an opinion of you; the opinion then becomes quite fixed. If you are wearing the right colours and have an image to suit your personality, the first impression will be positive, starting you off on the right footing.

Colour consultants are generally self-employed. They initially work for a particular company, where they are trained. The cost of the training varies, as do the length and quality. The course lasts for between one and two weeks, and the fee includes training and materials. After this you then start to build up your clientele. They will not, however, be regular, as most people only need to have one consultancy session.

The hours that you work are flexible and there is no minimum required. Basically you have to get yourself known locally. Consultants normally do this by marketing their services to businesses and other interested organizations. They may give talks to local groups at little or no charge in order to create interest and attract customers.

Obviously, if you have to give talks to groups and undertake marketing exercises you will need a high degree of personal confidence. Qualifications are not necessary, but a strong interest in colours and fashion is essential. Many people become involved in the business after a successful colour consultation of their own. Having reaped the benefits themselves, they wish to pass them on to others. It is essential for consultants to look the part: they need to be smart and very presentable. They also need to be able to relate well to people. Often a client may have to be told that he or she has been dressing in the wrong colour and style for years. The colour consultant must do this with sympathy and tact in order not to alienate or embarrass the client.

**Checklist of things to remember when looking for a company to train and work for**

1 What does the initial charge include? Can it be split, so that you can pay some of it when you start making money?

2 Does the training cover colour and image?

3 What part of your income goes to the parent company?

4 Is there a minimum amount of hours that you have to work?

5 Do you get any training on the difficulties and legal requirements of being self-employed?

6 Do you get any training in the art of public speaking?

7 Will there be an opportunity to accompany an experienced consultant to see how they operate as a public speaker?

8 Will you have the opportunity to work on live models during your training?

*I would suggest that before you make a final decision on a company, you check out its reputation. It may be a good idea to act as a customer to see how you feel about the services provided.*

### Jane comments on being a colour consultant

When I left school I took a secretarial course and then started work as a secretary. I didn't really enjoy the work but it was what most girls did. I left when my husband and I started a family. When my children began school full-time I went back to secretarial work as a temp. I had to do it on a temporary basis as I wanted to be available during the children's school holidays, so that I could spend time with them. I still did not enjoy the work.

I met the woman for whom I now work when I attended a colour consultation session. I was fascinated with the subject and became friends with Carolyn. Eventually, when she set up in business on her own I asked her if there were any opportunities for me. Carolyn trained me to be a colour and image consultant and I have not looked back since.

The training was very practical and covered all areas of the work including the public speaking element, which at the time scared me the most. In fact, I have found it quite easy; if you're interested in your subject it seems to come fairly naturally and is something you get used to if you already have a degree of personal confidence.

I initially wrote to all the women's groups in the area offering myself as a speaker at their meetings. That proved fairly successful and brought in business. I have now started making contact with local companies, because I feel they will be a good source of business. I should like to increase my male clientele and am looking for ways to do this.

I like the flexibility of the job. I can more or less work when I want to, which allows me to have the school holidays with my children. I am in charge of my diary, which is great. There is, however, a lot of work involved, and most of the talks I give are in the evenings. Added to this is the paperwork. I had no idea how much would be involved, but I spend a day each week at this to keep my books in order for the tax people.

I probably do two sessions a week with between five and seven people in each. It is important that you have a room in your house in which you can shut your client and yourself away. Some sessions are inevitably on a Saturday when the family are about. Your clients pay you quite a lot of money for your expertise and expect you to act in a professional way, which is difficult if your family are making demands of you.

# 18

# Cosmetic Sales

There are three ways in which people sell cosmetics. These are firstly working for a cosmetic house, usually based in a department store; secondly, working for a retailer selling numerous goods including cosmetics or for a chemist, working all the time on the cosmetic counter; and thirdly, working from home selling a particular brand of cosmetics in the vicinity.

## Cosmetic Houses

It is in this area that most people wishing to work with cosmetics prefer to be. It is thought of as the most glamorous area. Cosmetic houses are companies that manufacture the products: mainly make-up, perfumes and skin care products, among other things. They then employ staff to sell those products in retail outlets. Thus the ground floor of many large department stores accommodates numerous representatives from different cosmetic houses. The staff working on these counters are employed by the cosmetic houses themselves and not by the department store. They are interviewed by the cosmetic house and have to abide by their code of discipline, wearing the uniform and following set sales techniques.

The cosmetic sales staff do, however, have to work the same hours as other staff in the store; they also have to abide by the same rules and regulations. They are allowed similar benefits since they often get the same staff discounts as the regular store employees and are offered subsidized meals in the staff restaurant.

The role of the cosmetic house staff is often misunderstood by the general public. They are actually sales staff selling products. They have to have a good knowledge of all their company's products. They are not normally expected to know about products sold by their competitors. Neither are they experts in make-up techniques, as they seldom apply their customer's make-up. It is true that cosmetic houses often have promotions in particular stores which include the offer of a free make-up to prospective customers. In some cases, however, outside staff who specialize in this area of the work, especially employed beauticians for instance, may be brought in.

Cosmetic sales staff are expected to advise customers on the use and application of the products that they sell. They are also expected to give advice about the most appropriate product for any particular skin type, but generally speaking their training does not cover skin analysis in any great depth.

Cosmetic houses advertise their vacancies as and when they occur; they do not recruit at particular times of the year. They interview suitable applicants and offer them employment, usually stipulating in which store they will be based. They sometimes expect that staff will move to other stores within the region if staff shortages occur because of sickness or holidays. In reality this happens only rarely, and most staff tend to stay in the store to which they have been appointed and only move to other stores for promotion.

All new staff undertake a training programme of about one week so that they become familiar with the products and their application. When they arrive at the store they are given store training in order to be familiar with health, safety and till procedures.

Most cosmetic houses look for sales staff who will have an understanding of their customers. Because the products sold by cosmetic houses tend to be on the expensive side, the majority of the client group are middle-aged and relatively well off. Therefore the houses prefer applicants to be twenty years old or over, with previous sales experience. Naturally, if you have been selling make-up and other beauty products already, you will have an advantage over other applicants who have not. But any kind of retail experience is acceptable to most cosmetic houses.

There are some agencies which specialize in providing freelance staff to cosmetic houses. Houses will approach these agencies when they have staff shortages or require additional help, for example during the run-up to Christmas and while sales are on. These agencies are based in cities and large towns, and it is possible to register with them for temporary work. Once registered, there is no guarantee of continuous work, or in fact of any work at all, but you will probably be asked to work somewhere for a few days a week. The more experience you have, the more likely it is that you will be offered continuous work, but this will depend on the season. For more information about these agencies you should contact the Federation of Recruitment and Employment Services, who may be able to tell you about an agency in your area. Their address is at the end of this chapter, p.112. Working for an agency is attractive to people who do not wish to work full-time, as it is possible to turn down work or to specify times when you are not available.

# Retailing Cosmetics

Chemists and other retail outlets sell cosmetics. These retailers employ staff specifically to run the cosmetic counters, although other staff may occasionally work there. Each retail company has a different policy, and therefore if you decide to apply for such a job it would be worth asking for a full job description. It is possible to find cosmetic house staff in some larger chemists; they can be distinguished by their uniforms.

Product familiarity is an important issue for sales staff employed in these areas. They spend a lot of time liaising with the manufacturers' representatives who will call at the shop to take orders and to offer advice. Selling skills are essential in any aspect of retailing. For cosmetic sales it is also important to be well presented. If possible, it is good to wear some of the products to show the customer that you have confidence in what you sell.

Retailers advertise their vacancies in many different ways. Use the normal agencies (for example, the Careers Office, Jobcentre, etc.) and local newspapers to see what is available in your area.

# Working from Home

There are now many companies that sell cosmetics and their related products direct to customers at the door. Some of these companies are famous. They rely on local representatives to sell the products by using a catalogue and making monthly visits to their regular customers.

The companies do not pay their representatives a salary but allow them a commission on the sales they make. Therefore the more you sell, the greater your income. It is entirely up to you how much time and effort you put into selling the product; there are no targets to meet. However there are other employees of the company who will do their utmost to encourage you to increase your sales. They may offer you incentives so that if you do reach a specific sales figure you receive a prize – perhaps a free holiday for the best sales figure in the south of England, for example.

There will probably be regular meetings with other representatives, which you should attend in order that you can see new products, learn about special offers, and of course compare your sales with your colleagues.

It is not necessary to apply for this type of job. The companies like their representatives to be interested in their products, and an approach to a local representative should put you in touch with the area co-ordinator. Training takes place at the regular meetings and particular emphasis is placed on product knowledge.

Many successful representatives do go on to gain full-time employment with the company, acting as area co-ordinators.

**Where to find out more**

Federation of Recruitment and Employment Services Ltd
10 Belgrave Square
London SW1X 8PH

# Acknowledgements

The author and publishers thank the following for permission to reproduce illustrations:

pp. 11, 36–7, 93  Champneys College of Health and Beauty International Training School;

pp. 12, 71  London Institute of Beauty Culture;

pp. 18, 20, 21, 22–3, 28  London College of Fashion, Beauty Department;

pp. 24, 25, 96–7, 101  Complections Int. Ltd., London School of Make-up;

pp. 26, 47  Essanelle;

p. 44  Photograph by Richard Earney;

pp. 50–1  Champneys Health Resort at Tring;

p. 85  The International Institute of Reflexology.